PISA

Education in Eastern Europe and Central Asia

FINDINGS FROM PISA

This work is published under the responsibility of the Secretary-General of the OECD. The opinions expressed and arguments employed herein do not necessarily reflect the official views of the OECD or UNICEF, or of their respective member countries.

This document, as well as any data and any map included herein are without prejudice to and do not reflect a position on the part of the OECD or UNICEF on the legal status of or sovereignty over any territory, the delimitation of international frontiers and boundaries, or the name of any territory, city or area.

Please cite this publication as:
OECD/UNICEF (2021), *Education in Eastern Europe and Central Asia: Findings from PISA*, PISA, OECD Publishing, Paris, *https://doi.org/10.1787/ebeeb179-en*.

ISBN 978-92-64-71411-3 (print)
ISBN 978-92-64-93631-7 (pdf)

PISA
ISSN 1990-8539 (print)
ISSN 1996-3777 (online)

Photo credits: Cover © Jacob Lund/Shutterstock; © Tom Wang/Shutterstock; © Syda Productions/Shutterstock.

Corrigenda to publications may be found on line at: *www.oecd.org/about/publishing/corrigenda.htm*.
© OECD/UNICEF 2021

This work is available under the Creative Commons Attribution-NonCommercial-No Derivatives license 3.0 IGO (CC BY-NC-ND 3.0 IGO). For specific information regarding the scope and terms of the licence as well as possible commercial use of this work or the use of PISA data please consult Terms and Conditions on *http://www.oecd.org*.

Preface from UNICEF

A lack of education and learning opportunities continues to threaten the future of children in Europe and Central Asia. Across the region, 3.4 million children of primary and secondary school age are out of school, and an additional 19.5 million children in school do not reach the minimum level of proficiency in mathematics. This learning crisis has been further exacerbated by school closures at the height of the COVID-19 pandemic.

All too often, it is the most marginalised children – including those from minority groups and with disabilities – who bear the brunt of this crisis and are left behind, which widens educational inequality and learning gaps.

This new study, carried out jointly by UNICEF and the OECD, is a contribution to the efforts being made by countries in the region to bridge this gap and achieve inclusive and equitable quality education for all children across Eastern Europe and Central Asia. Drawing on the large-scale data collected by the OECD Programme for International Student Assessment (PISA) 2018 surveys, the study investigates the underlying challenges of promoting children's learning and skills development, and provides new knowledge on how we can collectively address the unmet learning needs of every child.

We hope that this study will contribute to the development of education systems that provide all children with quality learning and a chance to reach their full potential. UNICEF will continue to listen to the voices of children and work with governments, development partners, civil society organisations and the private sector to ensure that every child learns and acquires new skills for the future.

Afshan Khan
UNICEF Regional Director for Europe and Central Asia
Special Coordinator, Refugee and Migrant Response in Europe

Preface from the OECD

Countries in the Eastern Europe and Central Asia region (EECA) have ambitious aims to improve their economic competitiveness and civic participation. A highly skilled population is critical to creating the productive and modern economies and societies that these countries wish to build, which makes developing high-achieving and equitable education systems central to the future success of the region.

The OECD Programme for International Student Assessment (PISA) helps countries understand where they stand in terms of their educational outcomes. Results from EECA countries on PISA show that that the quality of education in the region has generally improved over time, though progress can still be made compared to countries across the OECD. Moreover, student outcomes vary greatly between and within countries; some students from the region are among the highest performing in the world while others are being left further behind.

Together with United Nations Children's Fund (UNICEF), the OECD is committed to supporting EECA countries and helping them achieve their economic and social goals. This comparative study builds upon the long-standing participation of EECA countries in PISA and the numerous education country reviews conducted by the OECD and UNICEF in the region. We analyse PISA data in detail to identify what the unique features of education in the region are and how they might shape student outcomes. Drawing upon our knowledge of education policy and practice in the region, we make recommendations that policymakers can consider when developing future educational reforms.

We hope that this study will not only be a useful resource for education systems in the EECA region, but will also further strengthen OECD's ties to the region and its valuable partnership with UNICEF.

Andreas Schleicher
Special Advisor on Education Policy to the Secretary-General
Director for Education and Skills

Table of contents

Preface from UNICEF	3
Preface from the OECD	4
Executive summary	8
1 Eastern Europe and Central Asia participation and outcomes in PISA 2018	**11**
Education in Eastern Europe and Central Asia	11
Purpose of this report and sources of evidence	11
Key features of Eastern Europe and Central Asian countries and their implications for student learning, as measured by PISA	15
Learning outcomes in Eastern Europe and Central Asia	19
References	33
Notes	34
2 Providing excellent and equitable schooling	**35**
Introduction	35
Student sorting and segregation	35
School resourcing	40
Learning time	51
Truancy	59
References	64
Note	67
3 Improving teaching	**69**
Introduction	69
Teaching practices	69
Teacher qualifications	76
Professional development	84
References	91
Notes	93

FIGURES

Figure 1.1. Average performance in Reading, Mathematics and Science	20
Figure 1.2. GDP per-capita and average reading performance	21
Figure 1.3. Proficiency levels in reading	23
Figure 1.4. Meta-cognitive skills	24

Figure 1.5. Average performance and within-country variation in reading — 25
Figure 1.6. Socio-economic status and reading performance — 26
Figure 1.7. Reading proficiency among students whose parents do not hold a higher education qualification — 27
Figure 1.8. Differences in reading performance by gender over time — 28
Figure 1.9. Average reading performance by school location — 29
Figure 1.10. Reading performance at the upper secondary level by educational tracks — 30
Figure 1.11. Profile of general and vocational students at the upper secondary level — 31
Figure 1.12. Language of instruction and reading performance — 32
Figure 2.1. The likelihood that low- and high-achieving students attend the same school — 38
Figure 2.2. Spending on education and average reading performance — 41
Figure 2.3. School technological infrastructure — 44
Figure 2.4. Principals' perceptions of material resources, by school socio-economic status and location — 46
Figure 2.5. Difference in computer-student ratio by type of school — 47
Figure 2.6. Learning time during regular school hours, by subject — 53
Figure 2.7. Total learning time in regular school lessons and reading performance — 53
Figure 2.8. Types of after-school language-of-instruction lessons offered at schools — 55
Figure 2.9. Percentage of students who attend schools that provide study help outside of regular school hours — 56
Figure 2.10. Learning time outside of school — 57
Figure 2.11. Learning time outside of school according to socio-economic quartiles — 58
Figure 2.12. Percentage of students who were truant in the two weeks prior to taking PISA — 60
Figure 2.13. Increased likelihood of student groups to be truant — 61
Figure 2.14. Difference in reading performance between the students with the most and least truant tendencies — 62
Figure 3.1. Teacher practices — 71
Figure 3.2. Teacher practices and reading performance — 72
Figure 3.3. Teacher behaviour that may hinder student learning — 73
Figure 3.4. Teacher qualifications — 78
Figure 3.5. Percentage of fully certified teachers, by school characteristics — 79
Figure 3.6. Percentage of teachers with at least a Master's degree, by school characteristics — 80
Figure 3.7. Teacher qualifications and reading outcomes — 81
Figure 3.8. Teacher qualifications and teacher practices — 82
Figure 3.9. Percentage of teachers who participate in professional development — 85
Figure 3.10. Participation in professional development by school type — 86
Figure 3.11. Professional development and teacher practices — 87
Figure 3.12. Use of student assessment to evaluate teachers — 89

TABLES

Table 1.1. Participation in PISA cycles — 13
Table 1.2. Aspects of PISA 2018 participation — 14
Table 1.3. Socio-economic indicators — 16
Table 1.4. Duration of compulsory education/training and student age groups, 2018-19 — 17
Table 1.5. Characteristics of the students in the PISA 2018 sample — 18
Table 1.6. PISA performance in reading over time — 19
Table 1.7. Summary description of the eight levels of reading proficiency in PISA 2018 — 22
Table 2.1. Criteria for admission into upper secondary education — 36
Table 2.2. Education system funding — 40
Table 2.3. Principal's perception of key educational resources — 43
Table 2.4. Principals' perceptions of technological infrastructure — 45
Table 2.5. Principals' perceptions of technological infrastructure in advantaged and disadvantaged schools — 48
Table 2.6. School resources and reading performance — 49
Table 3.1. Indices of teaching practice — 70
Table 3.2. Teacher standards in EECA countries — 75
Table 3.3. Requirements to become a fully certified teacher — 76

Follow OECD Publications on:

http://twitter.com/OECD_Pubs

http://www.facebook.com/OECDPublications

http://www.linkedin.com/groups/OECD-Publications-4645871

http://www.youtube.com/oecdilibrary

http://www.oecd.org/oecddirect/

This book has... *StatLinks*
A service that delivers Excel® files from the printed page!

Look for the *StatLinks* at the bottom of the tables or graphs in this book. To download the matching Excel® spreadsheet, just type the link into your Internet browser, starting with the *https://doi.org* prefix, or click on the link from the e-book edition.

Executive summary

The Eastern Europe and Central Asia[1] (EECA) region is undergoing rapid economic, social and political changes. While many countries in the region have made progress on several development indicators, they also face substantial challenges. Most countries are still struggling to attain the same level of development as international benchmarks, with per capita gross domestic product still well below the average across OECD countries. Economic inequality, as measured by the Gini coefficient, remains particularly high and/or is rising in many countries. Finally, good governance is an important issue and there is a recognized need to build trustworthy and effective systems in the region.

A knowledgeable and skilled population is a critical component to the vibrant economies and inclusive, cohesive societies that EECA countries aim to build, which makes education reform a central pillar of development efforts. To reform education, EECA countries need to understand the performance of their education systems and benchmark their outcomes against those of other countries. The OECD Programme for International Student Assessment (PISA) is a survey that assesses student learning and collects information about the characteristics of students and schools around the world. Many EECA countries have participated in PISA since its inception in 2000, and ten countries from the region did so in 2018, the widest participation to date. This report analyses PISA 2018 data to help determine what 15-year-olds in EECA countries know and can do. Based upon these findings, and drawing upon an international knowledge base that includes several United Nations Children's Fund (UNICEF)-OECD policy reviews, this report also suggests policy considerations about how education systems in the region can improve schooling and teaching to help all students learn and succeed.

Learning outcomes

Results from PISA 2018 reveal that overall outcomes from the region are improving. Many systems that participated in PISA prior to 2018 raised their performance in 2018 and none saw a decrease in performance. Simultaneously, EECA countries are now testing a greater share of 15-year-old students, which demonstrates that educational improvement and expansion are not mutually exclusive. Nevertheless, performance in EECA countries is generally lower than that of countries across the OECD. The EECA average in reading, the main domain assessed in PISA 2018, was 421 score points, compared with 487 in the OECD. Achievement within the region also varies greatly, with Georgia scoring 380 in reading and Croatia scoring 479.

Worryingly, PISA 2018 results also show that learning outcomes in the region are highly inequitable. Boys perform worse than girls at rates exceeding international averages. In systems with many rural schools,

---

[1] This report focuses on countries in Eastern Europe and Central Asia that are supported by the UNICEF ECARO office and participated in the OECD's Programme for International Student Assessment in 2018—Azerbaijan, Belarus, Bulgaria, Croatia, Georgia, Kazakhstan, Moldova, Romania, Turkey and Ukraine.

students from urban areas outperform students from rural areas at rates much greater than in similar OECD countries.

Providing excellent and equitable schooling

A key feature of education in the some parts of the EECA region is that enrolment into upper secondary education is very academically selective when compared to OECD countries. Relatedly, students in upper secondary schools are highly segregated; low- and high-achieving students are isolated from each other in many EECA countries, as are socio-economically disadvantaged and high-achieving students. Given the disparities in educational outcomes in some EECA countries, these findings raise questions about the equity of education systems in the region. Students from more advantaged backgrounds with stronger academic performance might compete for places in prestigious upper secondary schools, while students from more disadvantaged backgrounds and weaker academic performance might be grouped together in other institutions. Countries in the region are addressing these issues by improving the quality of education in lower levels of schooling, strengthening the value of all upper secondary education pathways and programmes and reforming selection mechanisms into upper secondary schools to focus less on examination results.

Another characteristic of education systems in EECA countries is their level and distribution of school resources. Compared to international benchmarks, education spending in the region is low, especially when considering the significant infrastructural improvements that many schools need. In addition, resource allocation is inequitable. Schools with more socio-economically advantaged student intakes tend to enjoy greater resourcing than schools with more disadvantaged student intakes, and urban schools are often better resourced than rural schools. These trends can exacerbate inequities, especially at the upper secondary level, as students from advantaged backgrounds might be selected into better-resourced schools than students from disadvantaged backgrounds. EECA countries can consider several strategies to address these concerns, such as establishing more equitable funding policies, improving school leaders' capacity to use resources, and strengthening school evaluation to better identify the needs of schools.

Compared to international benchmarks, students in EECA countries are provided with significantly less learning time during regular school hours (overall roughly two hours less per week than the OECD average, and as much as five hours less in some countries). On the other hand, learning time outside of school tends to be relatively higher in EECA countries, in particular participation in commercial tutoring. This situation is problematic because students might not have enough time in school to learn, but supplementing their learning outside of school is inequitable as students from advantaged backgrounds have access to more and higher quality resources. Allocating more learning time during regular school hours, and helping schools use the extra time wisely, can help address these inequities.

Finally, students in EECA countries generally show higher rates of truancy than their peers across the OECD. Roughly 60% of EECA students reported that they had been recently truant, compared to about 33% in OECD countries. Boys and disadvantaged students are more likely to be truant than girls and students from advantaged backgrounds. However, truancy in general has a weaker association with performance in the EECA region than across the OECD, which might reflect the lower levels of in-school learning time in the region and the higher levels of learning time outside of school. To address issues related to truancy, EECA countries can consider introducing data collection and analytical tools to identify truant students and develop programmes to target students who are most at risk of being truant and dropping out of school.

Assuring high quality teaching

Teaching is one of the most important aspects of an education system and can significantly shape student learning. In the EECA region, the teaching profession is influenced by several factors, including teachers' relatively older age and lower salaries compared to international benchmarks. Partly as a result of these factors, teaching practices in the region can be largely traditional and centred around the teacher (e.g. delivering a lecture to the whole class), with less emphasis on individualised, adaptive instruction. These circumstances might also contribute to inequities in learning, as teachers might not teach students from different backgrounds in ways that best help them learn. EECA teachers are also, on average, more likely to engage in negative behaviour such as not being prepared for classes or being absent from school. To improve this situation, EECA education systems have developed teacher standards that spell out how teachers are expected to teach. Using these standards to help determine career progression and professional development can further encourage teachers to implement the desired practices in their classrooms. EECA countries can also consider developing codes of conduct to more clearly set out what is expected of teachers in terms of their day-to-day practice, disposition and integrity.

Requirements related to teacher qualifications can help ensure high quality teaching. Teachers in EECA countries are fully certified and hold master's degrees at rates similar to teachers in OECD countries, though socio-economically advantaged and urban schools are more likely to have better qualified teachers. Unlike international benchmarks, however, teacher certification and holding advanced degrees are less positively associated with increased student performance or improved teacher practices, suggesting that these quality assurance mechanisms are not always fulfilling their purposes. EECA countries can consider introducing several measures to improve how well teacher qualifications signal high quality teaching. These initiatives include raising the quality of initial teacher education programmes, introducing measures to assure the quality of initial teacher education and implementing mandatory probation once teachers begin teaching. To make the allocation of qualified teachers more equitable, countries can create incentive schemes that better compensate teachers for working in environments that are more difficult.

To improve teacher practice, most education systems provide teachers with professional development that is based upon their observed needs. In EECA countries, teachers generally engage in less professional development than teachers across OECD countries, and those who work in socio-economically disadvantaged and rural schools are even less likely to do so. Moreover, more professional development in the region, unlike in OECD countries, is not associated with more frequent use of desired teaching practices, which suggests that there could issues be related to how teachers' needs are identified, and the quality of professional development opportunities. To expand professional development, EECA countries are providing more funding to schools and teachers, constructing training centres and better leveraging technology. To create higher quality training that is relevant to teachers, countries can consider accrediting training providers and making the teacher appraisal process more holistic, which can help form a more accurate understanding of what teachers' strengths and weaknesses are and what further training they might need.

1 Eastern Europe and Central Asia participation and outcomes in PISA 2018

Education in Eastern Europe and Central Asia

Countries in Eastern Europe and Central Asia[1] (EECA) have undergone tremendous social and political changes in the last 30 years. Most have transitioned from centralised and planned societies to market-based ones and economic development, as measured by gross domestic product (GDP) per-capita, has risen overall (World Bank, 2021[1]). Regional growth has been led by Bulgaria, Croatia and Romania, which have also acceded into the European Union. Other countries, such as Azerbaijan and Kazakhstan, have seen less consistent development from year to year, but still show positive economic progress.

Despite the overall economic growth of the region, EECA countries still face several common challenges. In most countries, the level of development is well below those of most OECD countries. Moreover, the increasing prosperity and wealth of the region has not been equally distributed. Economic inequality, as measured by the Gini coefficient, remains particularly high in Georgia and Romania, and is both higher than the OECD average and rising in Bulgaria and Turkey (World Bank, 2021[2]). Finally, good governance is a critical issue in the region and there is a recognised need to build trustworthy and effective systems of government, particularly in Belarus, Moldova and Ukraine (EU, 2020[3]).

Education is central to achieving regional development goals, as knowledgeable and skilled populations are important in creating dynamic, sustainable economies and inclusive, participatory societies. EECA countries have a strong educational tradition and have produced students who achieve top marks in international competitions. However, the focus on identifying and developing top performers can also divert attention and resources away from helping all students realise their potential. A higher share of EECA students, especially those from disadvantaged backgrounds, drop out before completing secondary school, and many who stay in school do not master the basic competences needed to lead productive lives (UNICEF, 2017[4]; OECD, 2019[5]). Addressing these challenges will be crucial to the region's future economic development and social cohesion.

Purpose of this report and sources of evidence

This report uses data from the OECD Programme for International Student Assessment (PISA), policy findings from the United Nations Children's Fund (UNICEF)-OECD country reviews and other international research to identify strengths and challenges that are common to EECA education systems, recognising that there is scope for further analysis on issues relevant to specific countries (Box 1.1). This report also compares the outcomes from EECA countries to global benchmarks, which can reveal the unique features of education in the region. This kind of multi-country analysis can help determine regionally relevant practices that can help improve student outcomes, particularly in secondary school.

> **Box 1.1. Areas for further analysis**
>
> This report focuses on insights from PISA that can help inform the most salient and common educational challenges facing the EECA region. In developing this report, several areas were identified that might benefit from further analysis, but are not addressed here because they do not concern all education systems in the region. For instance, PISA results typically highlight differences between public and private schools. However, across the region only 4% of students on average attend private schools. Similarly, PISA focuses on the differences in outcomes between non-immigrant and immigrant students, who represent 13% of PISA-participating students across the OECD, but only 3% of students in EECA countries. While these issues may be important in some systems (for example, 12% of 15-year-old students in Turkey attend private schools), they are not significant factors to the overall performance of the region.
>
> Other issues might be important in the region, but are not captured by PISA data. Students with disabilities, for example, are excluded from the PISA sample. Identifying different ethnic groups, in particular the Roma, is not possible in PISA. Nevertheless, countries need to understand these issues systemically, such as how to enable schools to support diverse students where they are concentrated. To aid these efforts, many countries analyse PISA data in association with national indicators and publish these results as part of their annual reporting and cyclical strategic planning. UNICEF and the OECD are currently working with Turkey to analyse which school and student characteristics are associated with differences in outcomes with a view to identifying policy interventions that can improve equity.

Participation in PISA

PISA is a triennial survey (due to the COVID-19 epidemic, PISA will be administered next in 2022) of 15-year-old students around the world. It assesses the extent to which they have acquired the knowledge and skills in reading, mathematics and science that are essential for full participation in social and economic life. PISA does not just assess what students know, but examines how well students can extrapolate from what they have learned and apply their knowledge in real-life settings.

In addition to benchmarking performance, PISA also collects a diverse array of information about students' families and their socio-economic background, which can be used to better understand the educational equity of countries. Since 2000 when two countries from the region took PISA, EECA countries have continuously increased their engagement and ten participated in 2018 (Table 1.1). Kyrgyzstan also participated in 2006 and 2009, while Mongolia and Uzbekistan are expected to participate in PISA 2022.

In 2018 the PISA assessment was computer-based in most countries (the transition to the computer-based assessment started in 2015), but was still paper-based in 9 out of 79 PISA-participating countries and economies, including Moldova, Romania and Ukraine (Table 1.2). Data between the two modes are comparable, but the paper-based assessment does not include interactive and adaptive items (OECD, 2019[5]).

All countries and economies in PISA 2018 distributed the student and school questionnaires and some participants also administered optional background questionnaires. These included questionnaires for students (about their educational careers, information and communication technology (ICT) familiarity, well-being and financial literacy), parents and teachers. Table 1.2 shows the optional questionnaires taken by EECA countries.

Table 1.1. Participation in PISA cycles

	Baku (Azerbaijan)	Belarus	Bulgaria	Croatia	Georgia	Kazakhstan	Moldova	Romania	Turkey	Ukraine
PISA 2000			X					X		
PISA 2003									X	
PISA 2006	X		X	X				X	X	
PISA 2009	X		X	X	X	X	X	X	X	
PISA 2012			X	X		X		X	X	
PISA 2015			X	X	X	X	X	X	X	
PISA 2018	X	X	X	X	X	X	X	X	X	X

Notes: Azerbaijan as a whole country participated in 2006 and 2009.
Bulgaria conducted the PISA 2000 assessment in 2001 and Romania in 2002, as part of PISA 2000+.
Georgia and Moldova conducted the PISA 2009 assessment in 2010 as part of PISA 2009+.
Kazakhstan participated also in 2015 but coverage was too small to ensure comparability, so the data were not published.

Table 1.2. Aspects of PISA 2018 participation

		Baku (Azerbaijan)	Belarus	Bulgaria	Croatia	Georgia	Kazakhstan	Moldova	Romania	Turkey	Ukraine
Computer format of the assessment		X	X	X	X	X	X			X	
Global competence assessment					X		X				
Financial literacy assessment/questionnaire				X		X					
Optional questionnaires	Educational Career			X	X		X				
	ICT			X	X	X	X			X	
	Parent				X	X					
	Teacher	X									
	Well-being			X		X					

Notes: The PISA assessment had a computer format in 70 countries/economies. The global competence assessment was conducted in 27 countries, the financial literacy assessment in 21, the educational career questionnaire in 31, the ICT questionnaire in 50, the parent questionnaire in 17, the teacher questionnaire in 19 and the well-being questionnaire in 9 countries.

Regional analyses

UNICEF and the OECD have regularly studied education in the EECA region. Since 2006, the UNICEF Europe and Central Asia Regional Office has conducted analysis of PISA results for several countries in the region. UNICEF and the OECD have recently completed education policy reviews on schooling for Romania (2017), Turkey (2019) and Georgia (2019). The OECD has also conducted reviews in Kazakhstan (2020, 2015 and 2014) and Ukraine (2017). These studies focused on policies related to evaluation and assessment, school resources, skills development, vocational education and integrity. In 2020, UNICEF and the OECD also developed a report based on PISA data for countries in the Western Balkans region. The knowledge base and analytical frameworks built by these activities greatly inform and shape this report.

Key features of Eastern Europe and Central Asian countries and their implications for student learning, as measured by PISA

In each participating country, PISA 2018 assessed a representative sample of children between the ages of 15 years and 3 months and 16 years and 2 months who were enrolled in an educational institution at Grade 7 or above. A two-stage sampling procedure selected a sample of at least 150 schools and roughly 42 students within each of those schools. The majority of countries assessed between 5 000 and 7 000 students. Kazakhstan tested roughly 20 000 students in order to produce representative results for each region. The national context of each country that participates in PISA affects greatly the students who are sampled to participate in the survey. This section discusses some of the key contextual features of EECA countries, and how these contexts are represented in their PISA 2018 student samples.

Socio-economic context

EECA countries have more socio-economically disadvantaged students compared to OECD countries

An important concern for all countries is how students from disadvantaged backgrounds perform compared to their advantaged peers, which helps indicate the extent to which the school system helps students overcome socio-economic inequalities. While there is variation between countries, EECA countries are, on average, lower income than those in the OECD. EECA countries had an average GDP per-capita of USD 20 839 (United States dollars) purchasing power parity (PPP) in 2018, compared to the OECD average of USD 44 994 (Table 1.3).

While wealth is an important measure of socio-economic status, other factors also influence a student's level of advantage. In PISA, a student's background is represented through the index of economic, social and cultural status (ESCS), which is created based upon information about a student's home environment, parents' level of education and parents' employment. This index is calculated such that the OECD average is 0.0 and one standard deviation is 1.0. The average ESCS across EECA countries is -0.4. However, there are disparities within the region. Belarus has an ESCS of 0.1, while Turkey has an average ESCS of -1.1. Since socio-economic context and student performance are closely related, it is important to consider these data when interpreting and comparing the educational outcomes of EECA countries.

Table 1.3. Socio-economic indicators

	Per-capita GDP in 2018 (PPP, USD)	PISA 2018 ESCS
Azerbaijan	14 556	-0.6
Belarus	19 345	0.1
Bulgaria	22 611	-0.3
Croatia	28 215	-0.2
Georgia	14 604	-0.4
Kazakhstan	26 167	-0.4
Moldova	12 674	-0.6
Romania	29 193	-0.5
Turkey	28 395	-1.1
Ukraine	12 629	-0.2
EECA average	20 839	-0.4
OECD average	44 994	0.0

Note: The data for this table were collected before Costa Rica became an OECD member.
Sources: The World Bank (n.d.[6]), *GDP per-capita (current international)*, https://data.worldbank.org/indicator/NY.GDP.PCAP.PP.CD (accessed 19 February 2021); (OECD, 2019[5]), *PISA 2018 Database*, https://www.oecd.org/pisa/data/2018database/ (accessed 17 November 2020).

StatLink https://stat.link/vtlzi0

A relatively higher share of students in EECA countries attend schools in rural areas

The EECA region is vast and includes a variety of communities from small, rural villages to large, urban cities. On average, the share of students who attend school in rural communities (defined as having populations of 3 000 people or fewer) is relatively larger across the EECA region (15% compared to 9% across the OECD), but some countries have considerably higher shares. In fact, Moldova (47%), Georgia and Kazakhstan (both 30%) are three of the four most rural countries that participate in PISA. Research has shown that rural schools can face several challenges, ranging from infrastructure to human resources (Echazarra and Radinger, 2019[7]). Where relevant (and focusing on countries with large shares of students who attend schools in rural areas), this report will explore how school location can shape student learning outcomes.

Educational landscape

PISA coverage rates vary in EECA countries

As PISA only assesses students attending an education institution, the learning outcomes of 15-year-olds who are out of school are not captured in PISA data. The share of the total population of 15-year-olds in a country that is eligible to participate in PISA is known as the coverage index. In some EECA countries, the general age at which compulsory education ends is 15 or earlier (Table 1.5). In these countries, some students might already have left school when PISA is administered, which can lower the countries' coverage indices. Other factors, such as a high rate of dropout or grade repetition, can also affect a country's coverage index.

Across EECA countries, the coverage index is slightly lower than the OECD average (80% compared to 88%) (Table 1.5). Disparities at the country-level are quite wide. While Kazakhstan and Moldova have coverage indices above 90%, Baku (Azerbaijan) has a coverage index of 46%, which is the lowest among all PISA-participating countries and reflects the relatively low leaving age. Readers of this report should interpret PISA results in light of these differences in coverage.

Table 1.4. Duration of compulsory education/training and student age groups, 2018-19

	Official entrance age to primary education (years), 2019	General leaving age
Azerbaijan	6	14
Belarus	6/7	14/15
Bulgaria	7	16
Croatia	6/7	15
Georgia	6	14
Kazakhstan	6	15
Moldova	7	16
Romania	6	17
Turkey	6	18
Ukraine	6	17

Notes: Grade that corresponds to end of compulsory education is from UNICEF-OECD country reviews.
Starting age refers to the official age at which students start compulsory education/training.
The possibility of early entry to primary education is not taken into account nor are the specific admission conditions of pupils officially recognised with special educational needs.
Leaving age refers to the statutory age at which students are expected to complete compulsory education/training.
Source: (UNESCO-UIS, 2021[8]), *UIS dataset*, http://data.uis.unesco.org/, (accessed 29 June 2021).

Students in EECA countries take PISA in both lower and upper secondary education

In some countries, 15-year-old students are transitioning from lower secondary to upper secondary education, which means that PISA participants in those countries are often from both these levels of education. In EECA countries, more students are in upper secondary education when they take PISA compared to the OECD average (76% vs 52%). Nevertheless, less than 62% of students in Baku (Azerbaijan), Belarus and Kazakhstan were in upper secondary education, and less than 10% of students in Moldova were. Which level students are in when they take PISA could affect their results. As mentioned previously, in many EECA countries compulsory education ends before upper secondary education, and thus upper secondary students may be a more self-selective group.

EECA countries generally track upper secondary students into general education and vocational pathways and more specific programmes

Many countries divide students into different types of educational pathways, or tracks. Among these pathways, the two most common are general education, which typically prepares students for academic tertiary studies, and vocational education, which equips students with practical skills to enter the workforce (in most countries vocational students can also enter tertiary education). Internationally, countries vary in terms of when students are selected into different tracks. While some systems, such as Austria, start sorting students after primary education, the majority start offering distinct tracks to students at the beginning of upper secondary school.

In the EECA region, 28% of upper secondary students are enrolled in a vocational pathway (compared to 21% across the OECD) but the size and nature of vocational sectors varies greatly across countries. Although in Baku (Azerbaijan), Georgia and Moldova have almost no students in vocational pathways, 49% of students in Bulgaria and 68% of students in Croatia are enrolled in vocational pathways at the upper secondary level. In Kazakhstan, a sizeable vocational sector operates, but is considered largely separate from the upper secondary education system and is often classified at ISCED 4 and 5 levels. A distinguishing feature of EECA education systems is that many select students into specific programmes within pathways (e.g., general education schools that specialise in mathematics). Chapter 2 of this report explores issues around student grouping and segregation in greater depth.

Table 1.5. Characteristics of the students in the PISA 2018 sample

	Baku (Azerbaijan)	Belarus	Bulgaria	Croatia	Georgia	Kazakhstan	Moldova	Romania	Turkey	Ukraine	EECA average	OECD average
Number of students	6 827	5 803	5 294	6 609	5 572	19 507	5 367	5 075	6 890	5 998	-	-
Percentage of the 15-year-old population covered by the PISA sample (Coverage Index 3)	46	88	72	89	83	92	95	73	73	87	80	88
Modal grade (grade most represented by 15-year-olds)	Grade 10	Grade 10	Grade 9	Grade 9	Grade 10	Grade 10	Grade 9	Grade 9	Grade 10	Grade 10	-	-
Share in upper secondary education	62	56	100	100	85	54	10	93	99	100	76	52
Students' PISA index of economic, social and cultural status	-0.6	-0.1	-0.3	-0.2	-0.4	-0.4	-0.6	-0.5	-1.1	-0.2	-0.4	0.0
Share of girls	47	48	47	50	48	49	49	48	50	47	48	50
Share of students with an immigrant background	5	4	1	9	1	8	1	1	1	2	3	13
Share of students who speak the test language at home	89	96	87	97	94	90	91	97	93	64	90	88
Share of students enrolled in vocational programmes — All students	0	14	49	67	0	20	3	12	33	28	23	12
Share of students enrolled in vocational programmes — Students in upper secondary education	0	25	49	68	0	36*	-	13	33	28	28	21
Share of students enrolled in schools located in: A village or rural areas (fewer than 3 000 people)	1	17	3	1	30	30	47	7	1	19	15	9
Share of students enrolled in schools located in: Towns (from 3 000 to about 100 000 people)	52	33	57	59	23	19	32	53	32	34	40	53
Share of students enrolled in schools located in: Cities (over 100 000 people)	47	50	40	40	47	51	21	40	67	47	45	38
Share of students in private schools	0	0	1	2	11	8	1	2	12	1	4	18

* Classified as ISCED 5

Note: The data for this table were collected before Costa Rica became an OECD member.
Source: (OECD, 2019[5]), PISA 2018 Database, https://www.oecd.org/pisa/data/2018database/ (accessed 17 November 2020).

Learning outcomes in Eastern Europe and Central Asia

Overall performance

PISA results show that student outcomes in some EECA countries have improved over time. In Moldova and Turkey, student outcomes in reading have improved between the first year the countries participated and 2018. These countries have also increased their coverage indices, showing that gains in educational access and learning outcomes are not mutually exclusive (Table 1.6) (also see Box 1.3 for a discussion on how rising coverage indices might be reflected in different countries).

In other countries, student outcomes in reading have not changed between the first year they participated in PISA and 2018. From cycle to cycle, however, some differences can be observed. Georgia, for instance, improved in reading from an average of 374 score points in 2009 to 401 in 2015, before declining to 380 in 2018. On the other hand, outcomes in Bulgaria decreased from 430 on average in 2000 to 402 in 2006, before increasing in subsequent years[2].

Table 1.6. PISA performance in reading over time

	Score points in earliest year of availability	Score points in 2018	Coverage index in earliest year of availability	Coverage index in 2018
Bulgaria	430 (2000)	420	83% (2006)	72%
Croatia	477 (2006)	479	85% (2006)	89%
Georgia	374 (2009)	380	76% (2009)	83%
Kazakhstan	390 (2009)	387	89% (2009)	92%
Moldova	**388 (2009)**	**424**	90% (2009)	95%
Romania	428 (2000)	428	66% (2006)	73%
Turkey	**441 (2003)**	**466**	36% (2003)	73%

Notes: Bulgaria and Romania conducted the PISA 2000 assessment in 2001 as part of PISA 2000+. Georgia and Moldova conducted the PISA 2009 assessment in 2010 as part of PISA 2009+.
Statistically significant performance differences are represented in bold.
Coverage index refers to the percentage of the 15-year-old population represented in a country's PISA sample.
Data for the coverage index were not available before 2003.
Source: (OECD, 2019[5]), *PISA 2018 Database*, https://www.oecd.org/pisa/data/2018database/ (accessed 17 November 2020).

StatLink https://stat.link/x0t8rn

Though results in the region are generally improving, overall outcomes in the EECA region are still lower than international benchmarks (Figure 1.1). All countries in the region performed below the OECD average in reading, mathematics and science, though there is considerable variation. Students in Belarus and Croatia perform similarly to OECD countries such as Italy and Latvia. Meanwhile, Georgia and Kazakhstan perform similarly to lower-middle income countries like Panama and Thailand.

Figure 1.1. Average performance in Reading, Mathematics and Science

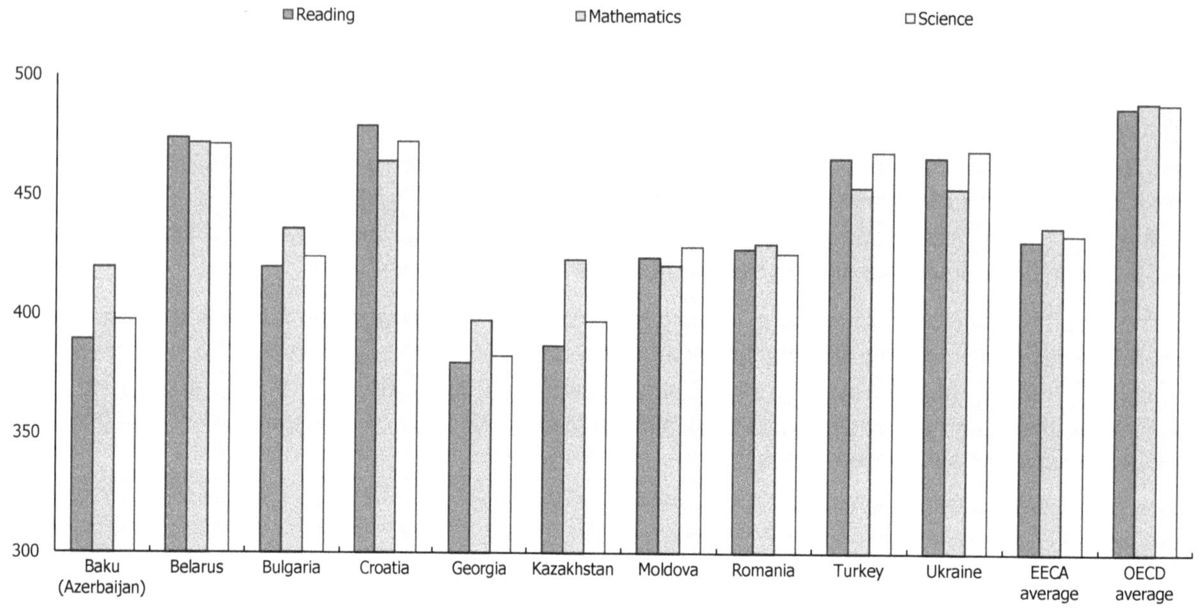

Note: The data for this figure were collected before Costa Rica became an OECD member.
Source: (OECD, 2019[5]), *PISA 2018 Database*, https://www.oecd.org/pisa/data/2018database/ (accessed 17 November 2020).

StatLink https://stat.link/nys7t6

As mentioned previously, one should interpret PISA results in light of participants' economic development, as 44% of performance differences in mean reading scores between countries in PISA 2018 can be accounted for by national income (OECD, 2019[5]). Figure 1.2 shows the performance of education systems relative to their per-capita GDP. In general, education systems in the EECA region perform around what would be predicted by their levels of economic development. However, some countries perform higher relative to others with similar income levels. Ukraine for example, performs better than several wealthier countries, which indicates the potential for policy to help overcome resource limitations.

Figure 1.2. GDP per-capita and average reading performance

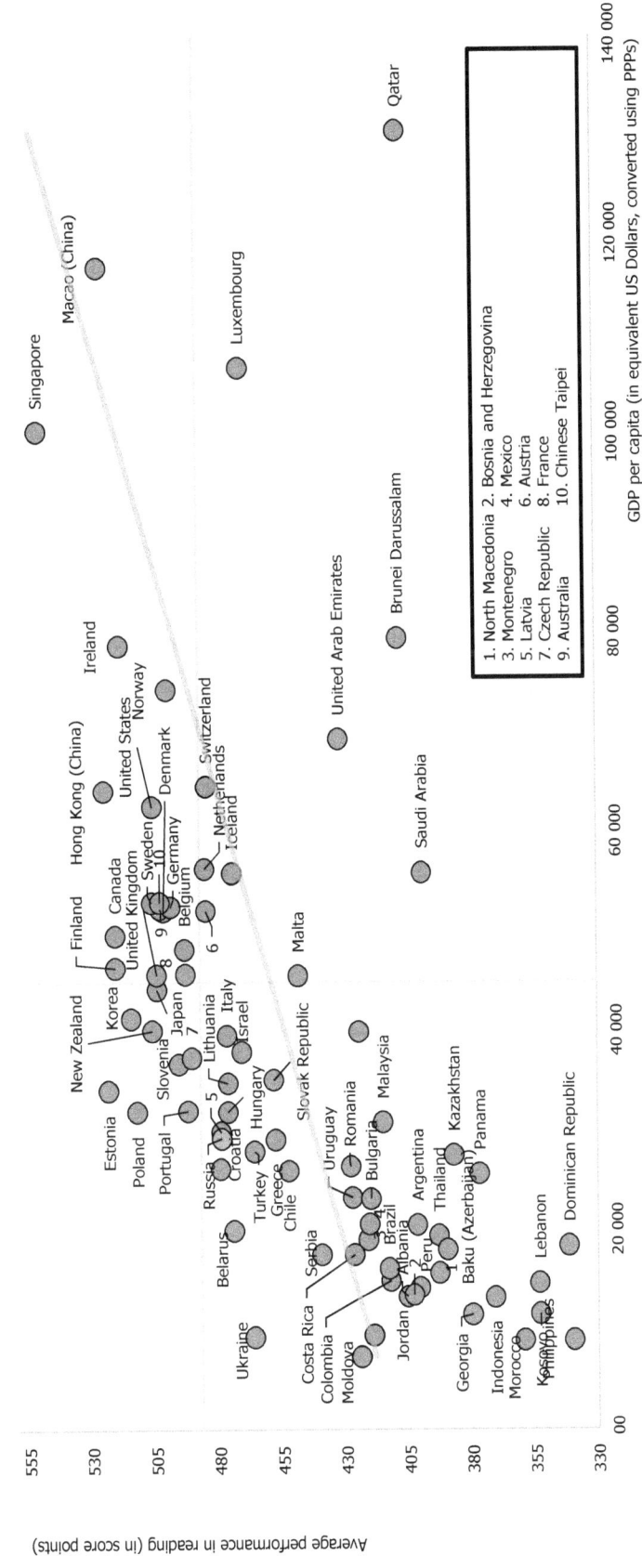

Notes: EECA economies are marked and labelled in red. Green lines indicate the OECD average. The data for this figure were collected before Costa Rica became an OECD member.
Sources: (OECD, 2019[5]), *PISA 2018 Database*, https://www.oecd.org/pisa/data/2018database/ (accessed 17 November 2020); World Bank (n.d.[6]), *GDP per-capita (current international $)*, https://data.worldbank.org/indicator/NY.GDP.PCAP.PP.CD (accessed 10 February 2021).

StatLink https://stat.link/pmny1q

To help understand differences in student knowledge and skills, PISA categorises student performance into different proficiency levels. These levels in reading, which was the main assessment domain in PISA 2018, range from the highest (Level 6) to the lowest (Level 1c) proficiency (Table 1.7). Level 2 is considered the minimum level of proficiency students need to acquire to advance in their education and participate in modern societies.

Table 1.7. Summary description of the eight levels of reading proficiency in PISA 2018

Level	Lower score limit	Percentage of students able to perform tasks at each level or above (OECD average)	Characteristics of tasks
6	698	1.3%	Readers at Level 6 can comprehend lengthy and abstract texts in which the information of interest is deeply embedded and only indirectly related to the task. They can compare, contrast and integrate information representing multiple and potentially conflicting perspectives, using multiple criteria and generating inferences across distant pieces of information to determine how the information may be used.
5	626	8.7%	Readers at Level 5 can comprehend lengthy texts, inferring which information in the text is relevant even though the information of interest may be easily overlooked. They can perform causal or other forms of reasoning based on a deep understanding of extended pieces of text. They can also answer indirect questions by inferring the relationship between the question and one or several pieces of information distributed within or across multiple texts and sources, and can establish distinctions between content and purpose, and between fact and opinion.
4	553	27.6%	At Level 4, readers can comprehend extended passages in single or multiple-text settings. They interpret the meaning of nuances of language in a section of text by taking into account the text as a whole. In other interpretative tasks, students demonstrate understanding and application of ad hoc categories. They can compare perspectives and draw inferences based on multiple sources.
3	480	53.6%	Readers at Level 3 can represent the literal meaning of single or multiple texts in the absence of explicit content or organisational clues. Readers can integrate content and generate both basic and more advanced inferences. They can also integrate several parts of a piece of text in order to identify the main idea, understand a relationship or construe the meaning of a word or phrase when the required information is featured on a single page.
2	407	77.4%	Readers at Level 2 can identify the main idea in a piece of text of moderate length. They can understand relationships or construe meaning within a limited part of the text when the information is not prominent by producing basic inferences, and/or when the text(s) include some distracting information.
1a	335	92.3%	Readers at Level 1a can understand the literal meaning of sentences or short passages. Readers at this level can also recognise the main theme or the author's purpose in a piece of text about a familiar topic, and make a simple connection between several adjacent pieces of information, or between the given information and their own prior knowledge.
1b	262	98.6%	Readers at Level 1b can evaluate the literal meaning of simple sentences. They can also interpret the literal meaning of texts by making simple connections between adjacent pieces of information in the question and/or the text.
1c	189	99.9%	Readers at Level 1c can understand and affirm the meaning of short, syntactically simple sentences on a literal level, and read for a clear and simple purpose within a limited amount of time.

Source: (OECD, 2019[5]), *PISA 2018 Database*, https://www.oecd.org/pisa/data/2018database/ (accessed 17 November 2020).

Figure 1.3 shows that on average in the EECA countries, 42% of 15-year-old students did not attain the baseline proficiency level in reading (vs. 23% in the OECD). These students cannot identify the main idea of a text of moderate length, find information based on explicit, but sometimes complex, criteria, and reflect on the purpose and form of texts when explicitly directed to do so. However, there are large differences between countries in the region: Belarus, Croatia, Turkey and Ukraine were close to the OECD average, with about one student in four not reaching this baseline level. On the other hand, in Baku (Azerbaijan), Georgia and Kazakhstan, more than 60% of students do not reach this level.

Figure 1.3. Proficiency levels in reading

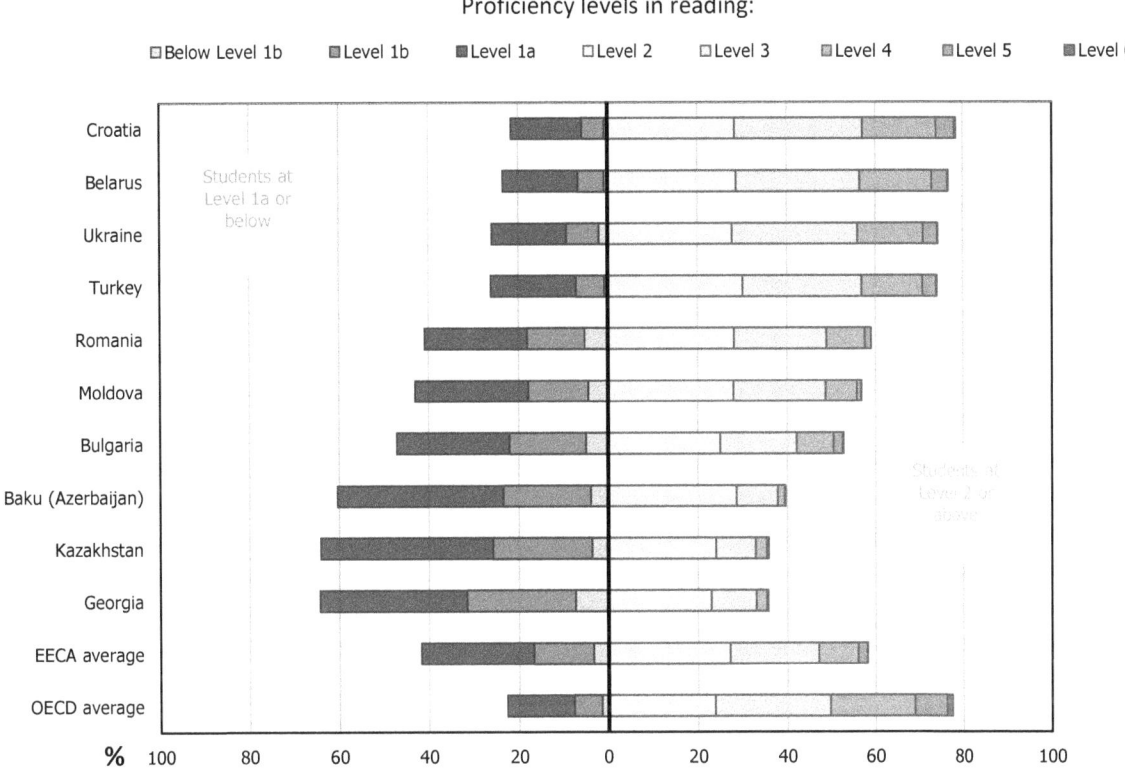

Notes: Countries are sorted by the percentage of students below Level 2 in reading.
The data for this figure were collected before Costa Rica became an OECD member.
Source: (OECD, 2019[5]), *PISA 2018 Database*, https://www.oecd.org/pisa/data/2018database/ (accessed 17 November 2020).

StatLink https://stat.link/o5gack

Box 1.2. Meta-cognitive skills

In addition to measuring students' reading literacy in general, PISA 2018 measured a specific set of reading skills, called meta-cognitive skills. PISA 2018 defines meta-cognitive skills as knowing how to guide one's own understanding and learn in different contexts. Having meta-cognitive skills is crucial in modern societies because they help individuals navigate, interpret and solve unanticipated problems. To measure meta-cognitive skills, PISA asked students about the usefulness of various strategies (understanding and remembering; summarising; assessing credibility) for accomplishing different types of reading tasks and compared their responses to those given by a group of experts. All EECA countries except Ukraine are below the OECD average in terms of students' meta-cognitive skills, and some by considerable margins (Figure 1.4)

Students in the region generally struggle more when asked to choose the best strategies for assessing the credibility of a source (especially in Baku (Azerbaijan) and Kazakhstan) and when summarising information. For example, PISA asked students what is an appropriate response to receiving an email from a mobile phone operator informing them that they have won a smartphone. EECA students were more likely to say that clicking on the associated link and filling out an online form was appropriate.

Students from OECD countries were more likely to be sceptical of such an offer, saying that they would check the website of the mobile phone operator to see if the offer is mentioned or delete the email without clicking on the link. This finding has economic and social implications, as it suggests that students from the region might be less discerning and critical of the information that they access.

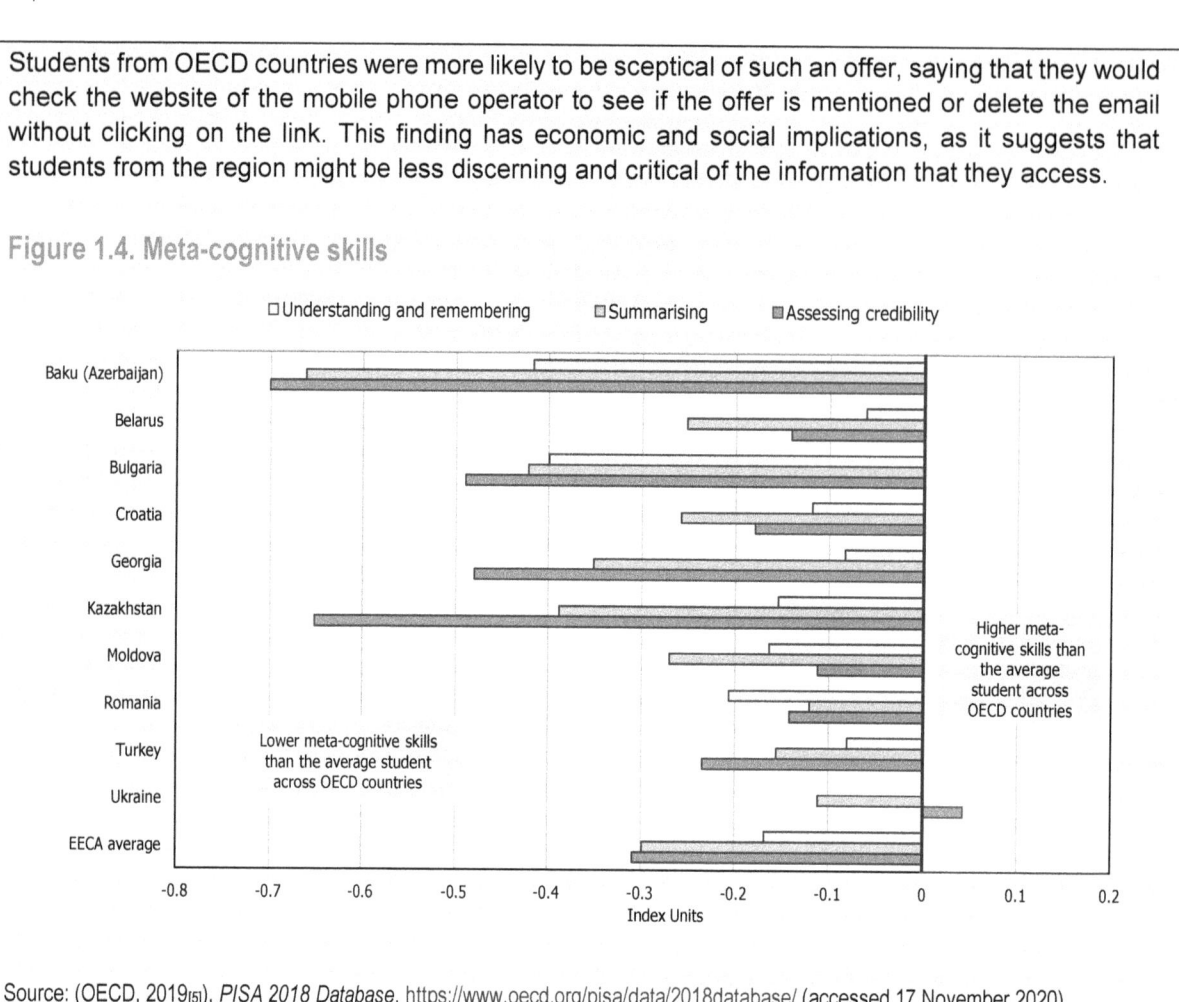

Figure 1.4. Meta-cognitive skills

Source: (OECD, 2019[5]), *PISA 2018 Database*, https://www.oecd.org/pisa/data/2018database/ (accessed 17 November 2020).

StatLink https://stat.link/z8fmxw

Performance and equity

In addition to overall performance, PISA measures the outcomes of different student groups within an education system. This type of disaggregation helps policy makers understand if all students are achieving similar outcomes, or if some students are performing very well while others are falling behind. This report concentrates primarily on equity according to students' socio-economic status, gender and, where relevant, school location (in a rural or urban area), which are important issues in the EECA region.

Figure 1.5 shows that, when looking across all PISA-participating economies, there is a strong, positive relationship between overall performance and variation in performance, likely owing to the wider range of possible student outcomes in higher performing countries. As EECA countries typically have lower performance compared to the OECD average, disparities between student groups in EECA countries might be smaller in absolute terms, but that does not mean these gaps are less meaningful. Readers should keep this information in mind as they interpret the PISA results. Where appropriate, this report will also report results in terms of country-level standard deviations to help contextualise comparison.

Figure 1.5. Average performance and within-country variation in reading

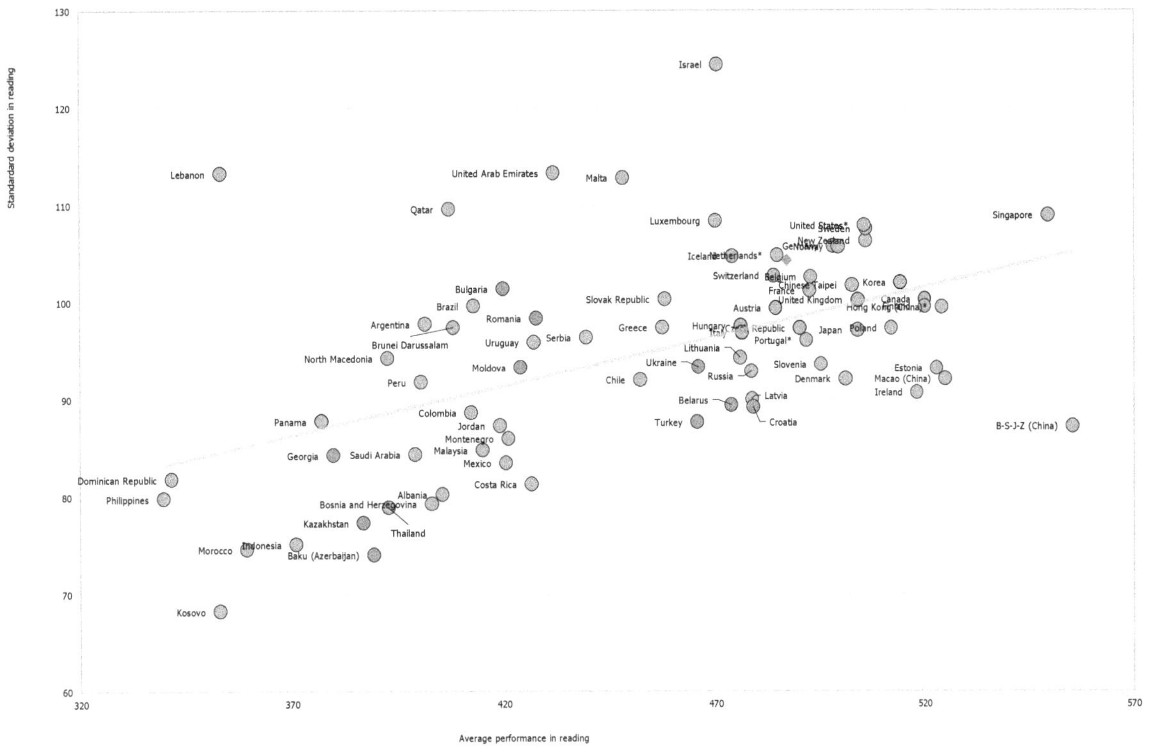

Source: (OECD, 2019[5]), *PISA 2018 Database*, https://www.oecd.org/pisa/data/2018database/ (accessed 17 November 2020).

StatLink https://stat.link/8yk61s

Socio-economic status

Socio-economically advantaged students[3] perform better on PISA than disadvantaged students in all PISA-participating countries and economies. On average across EECA countries, socio-economically advantaged students score 80 points more than socio-economically disadvantaged students (the gap across OECD countries is 89). Such gaps are highest in Romania (109) and Bulgaria (106), and lowest in Baku (Azerbaijan) (41) and Kazakhstan (40).

Figure 1.6. Socio-economic status and reading performance

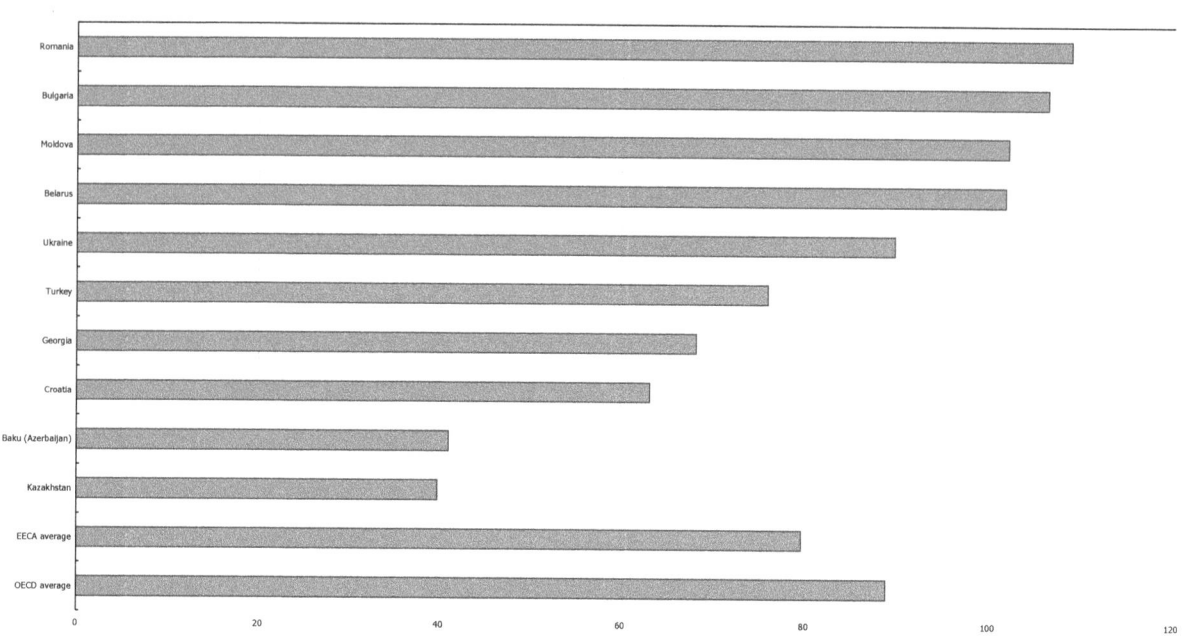

Notes: Countries are sorted by the difference in reading score. All differences are statistically significant.
The coverage index for Baku (Azerbaijan) was only 46%, so many 15-year-olds with a disadvantaged background will not even have been at school and do not appear here: the relationship between socio-economic status and performance may have been greater if it could have been observed on the entire 15-year-old population (OECD, 2019, p. 56[9]).
The data for this figure were collected before Costa Rica became an OECD member.
Source: (OECD, 2019[5]), *PISA 2018 Database*, https://www.oecd.org/pisa/data/2018database/ (accessed 17 November 2020).

StatLink https://stat.link/pca3d1

Box 1.3. Performance and participation of vulnerable students over time

As indicated in Table 1.6, in many EECA countries the share of students who are eligible to participate in PISA (coverage index) has increased over time. Increased coverage generally means that an education system is enrolling more students from disadvantaged backgrounds who may face more obstacles to learning (for example, less support from less educated parents), which can influence a country's overall outcomes (OECD, 2019[9]). However, specific changes in the composition of the student sample can differ according national contexts, and these differences can also shape how changes in overall performance are interpreted.

Figure 1.7 shows the change in the population of sampled students whose parents do not hold a higher education qualification, and the change in their achievement. These students were selected for further analysis because they are more likely not to be in school, and thus less likely to be covered in the

PISA sample. Furthermore, the definition of higher education qualification is consistent over time and thus the numbers of students from this group are comparable across years.

Figure 1.7. Reading proficiency among students whose parents do not hold a higher education qualification

Sample is restricted to students whose parents do not hold a higher education qualification

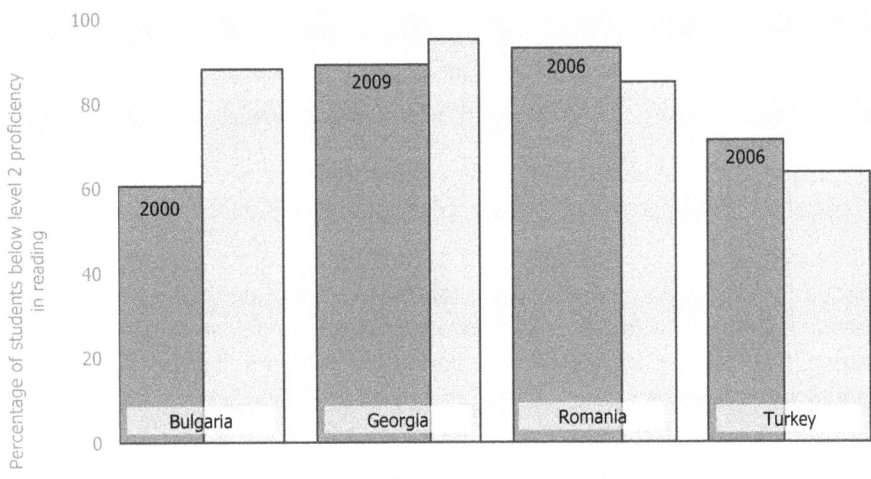

Notes: The width of the columns represents the number of students whose parents do not hold a higher education qualification and are scaled to be proportionate within each country.
The area of each column represents the number of students whose parents do not hold a higher education qualification who performed below Level 2 proficiency in reading.
Data from Bulgaria and Romania are from 2006 because coding for parental education was different in 2000, when they first participated. The four countries are selected because their coverage indices in 2018 were below that of the OECD average. Baku (Azerbaijan) is excluded because it did not previously participate as a municipality.
Sources: (OECD, 2019[5]), *PISA 2018 Database*, https://www.oecd.org/pisa/data/2018database/ (accessed 17 November 2020); (World Bank, 2021[1]), *Data Bank*, https://data.worldbank.org/indicator/SE.TER.CUAT.BA.ZS?end=2017&locations=GE-RO&start=1975&view=chart (accessed 26 June 2021).

StatLink https://stat.link/ucgdxh

Changes in the achievement of this student group vary across the analysed countries. In Bulgaria and Georgia, a greater share of sampled students achieved below Level 2 proficiency in reading in 2018 than in 2006 and 2009, respectively. These results suggest that these countries might not be effectively supporting vulnerable students, despite there being no significant increase in the number of such students, or even a decrease as in the case of Georgia. In Romania and Turkey, a smaller share of students whose parents do not hold a higher education qualification now achieve below Level 2 proficiency in reading, which indicates that these countries might be targeting more support at potentially vulnerable students. The situation is particularly noteworthy in Turkey given that the country also increased its population of such students.

The factors explaining the changes over time in the share of students whose parents do not hold a higher education qualification vary considerably across countries. In Georgia and Romania, the population of students whose parents do not hold a higher education qualification have decreased considerably, even though coverage indices increased, which is likely related to the increasing share of adults with a higher education qualification in these countries. In Bulgaria, the number of students from this group remained constant even though the coverage index decreased, which might be explained by high rates of brain drain (upcoming review). In Turkey, where compulsory education was extended to 12 years in 2011 (see Chapter 2), the coverage index doubled and the number of students in the PISA sample whose parents do not hold a higher education qualification increased

Gender

PISA results consistently show that girls tend to outperform boys by about 30 points in reading. In mathematics, boys outperform girls by roughly 5 points, and differences in science are not significant on average. In EECA countries, girls outperform boys by 32 points on average in reading in PISA 2018, which is similar to the difference across the OECD (30 points on average). Like OECD countries, there is considerable variation across countries. Six EECA countries have gender gaps greater than the OECD average, with the highest in Moldova and Bulgaria (40 score points). However, in terms of standard deviations, eight out of ten EECA countries have a larger gap than the OECD average.

Performance differences according to gender have decreased over time. Six out of eight countries in the region have reduced their gender gaps between their first years of participation and 2018 (Figure 1.8). These decreases were often because boys increased in performance while girls decreased, which was the case in Croatia, Georgia and Kazakhstan. In Bulgaria, both boys and girls decreased in performance, but girls decreased more than boys.

Figure 1.8. Differences in reading performance by gender over time

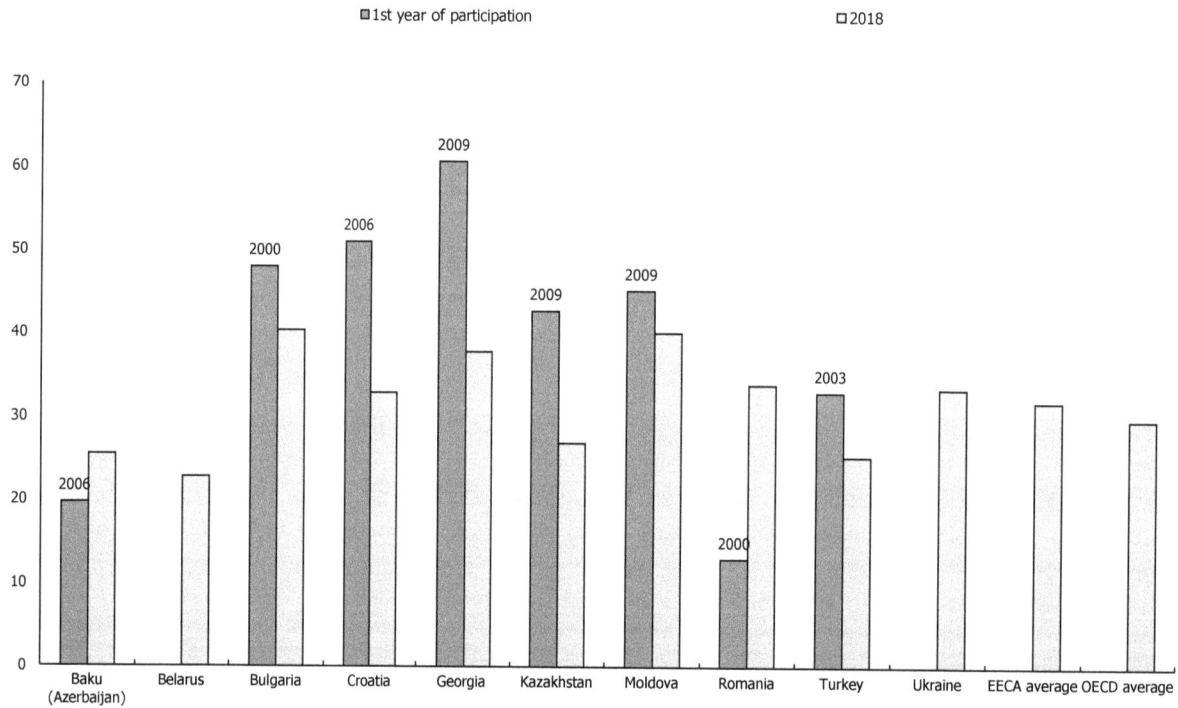

Notes: In 2006, Azerbaijan participated in PISA as a country. The data for this figure were collected before Costa Rica became an OECD member.
Source: (OECD, 2019[5]), *PISA 2018 Database*, https://www.oecd.org/pisa/data/2018database/ (accessed 17 November 2020).

StatLink ᐅ https://stat.link/i5mloj

School location

In most PISA-participating countries and economies, students enrolled in urban areas have higher performance than students in rural schools (OECD, 2019[9]). Among EECA countries where more than 3% of 15-year-old students were enrolled in rural schools, the urban-rural gaps in Moldova (89 points) and Romania (110 points) are considerably larger than the same gap across the OECD (35 points) (Figure 1.9). In terms of standard deviations, Kazakhstan's gap (0.55 standard deviations) is also larger than that of the OECD (0.51 standard deviations). After accounting for student and school socio-economic status, the relationship between geography and performance weakens but remains statistically significant in Georgia, Kazakhstan and Moldova.

Figure 1.9. Average reading performance by school location

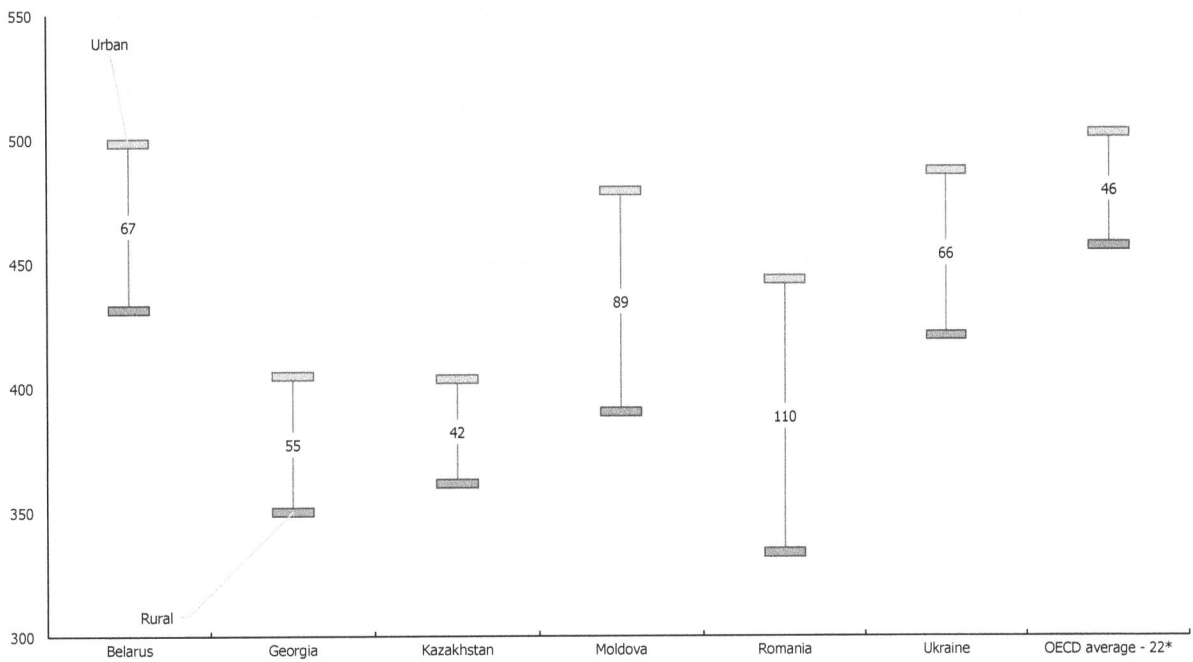

* Includes only the 22 OECD countries with more than 3% of students in rural schools.
Notes: From principals' reports on community in which their school is located.
Baku (Azerbaijan), Bulgaria, Croatia and Turkey have few 15-year-olds in rural schools (3% or less) so are not included in the figure.
The data for this figure were collected before Costa Rica became an OECD member.
Source: (OECD, 2019[5]), *PISA 2018 Database*, https://www.oecd.org/pisa/data/2018database/ (accessed 17 November 2020).

StatLink https://stat.link/fg3i2y

Educational tracks

Like in OECD countries, reading performance in EECA also varies according to education tracks, and gaps in three EECA countries are as large or larger than the OECD average (Figure 1.10). In terms of standard deviations, however, five EECA countries have gaps as large or larger than the OECD average, with only Kazakhstan and Ukraine having smaller differences. The observed gap in learning achievement between general and vocational pathways reflects not only a difference in curriculum but also a difference in student intake. Boys and socio-economically disadvantaged students are more likely to be enrolled in vocational programmes in all EECA countries where such tracks are offered (see Figure 1.11). These data suggest that student grouping and tracking in EECA countries reflect educational inequities at lower levels of education, and, without careful interventions, could risk exacerbating them.

Figure 1.10. Reading performance at the upper secondary level by educational tracks

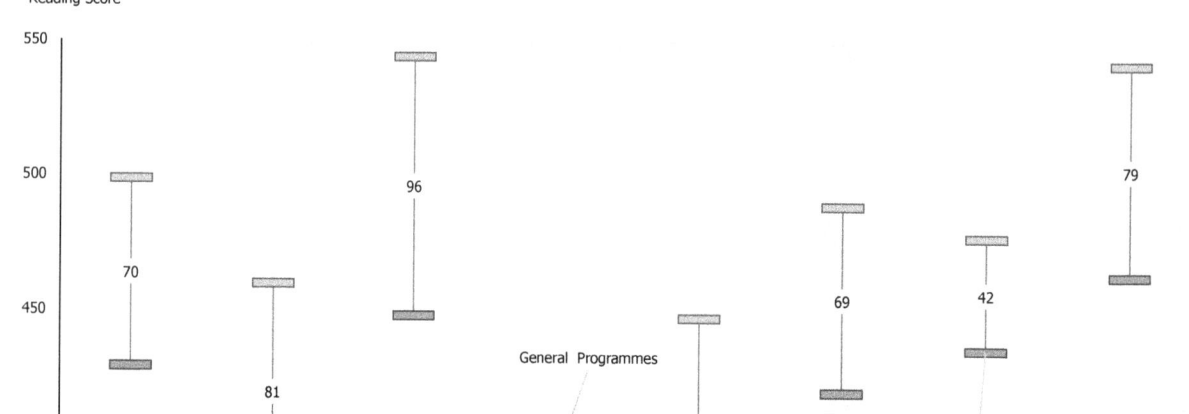

* Includes only the 23 OECD countries with at least 3% of students in vocational/pre-vocational schools.
Notes: In Moldova most 15-year-old students are at the lower secondary level and in Baku (Azerbaijan) and Georgia there are few vocational students at the upper secondary level, so they are not included in the figure.
The data for this figure were collected before Costa Rica became an OECD member.
Source: (OECD, 2019[5]), *PISA 2018 Database*, https://www.oecd.org/pisa/data/2018database/ (accessed 17 November 2020).

StatLink https://stat.link/np894e

Figure 1.11. Profile of general and vocational students at the upper secondary level

Difference in the share of students in vocational pathways by:

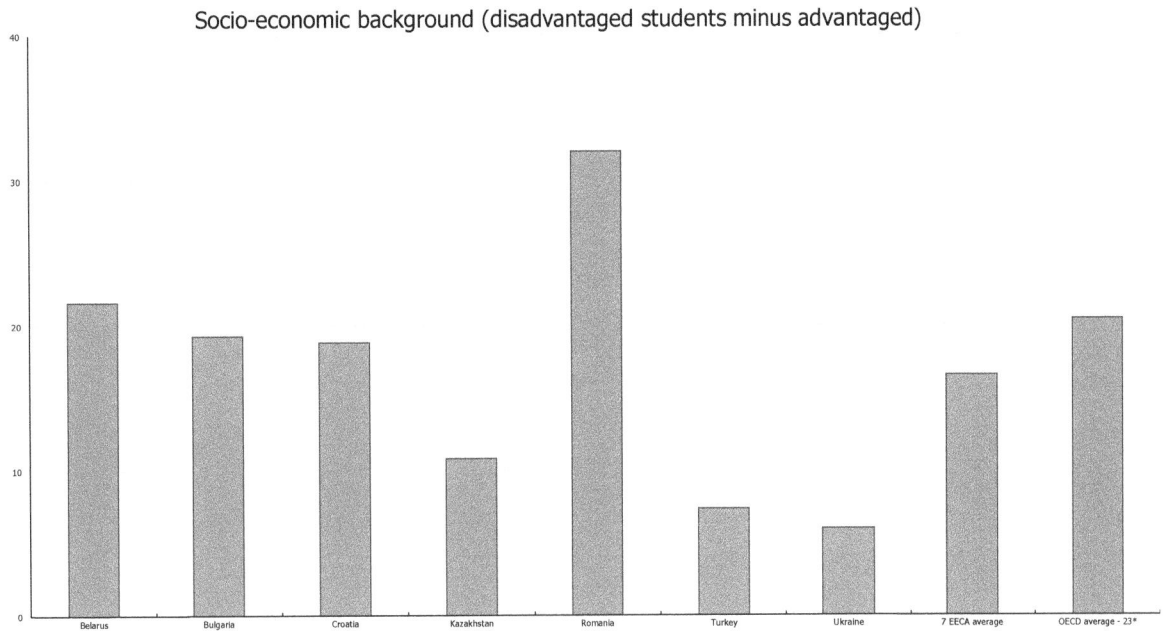

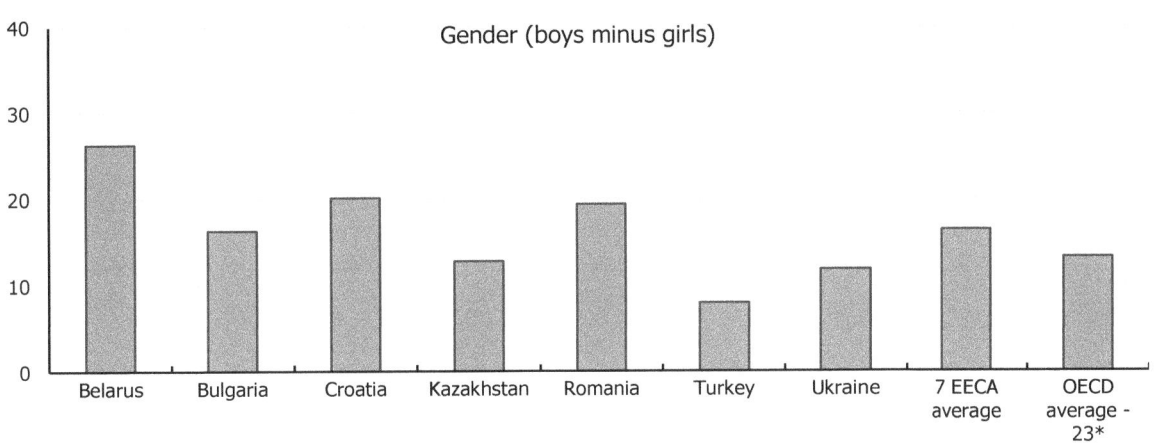

* Includes only the 23 OECD countries with at least 3% of students in vocational/pre-vocational schools.
Notes: In Moldova most 15-year-old students are at the lower secondary level and in Baku (Azerbaijan) and Georgia there are no separate general and vocational programmes even at the upper secondary level, so they are not included in the figure.
The data for this figure were collected before Costa Rica became an OECD member.
Source: (OECD, 2019[5]), *PISA 2018 Database*, https://www.oecd.org/pisa/data/2018database/ (accessed 17 November 2020).

StatLink https://stat.link/kgb03t

Box 1.4. Language of instruction

In Baku (Azerbaijan), Kazakhstan, Moldova and Ukraine, school instruction occurs in Azerbaijani, Kazakh, Romanian and Ukrainian, respectively, and also Russian in each country. PISA 2018 data were analysed to better understand if there are differences in learning outcomes according to students' languages of instruction (and, by proxy, the schools that instruct in those languages).

For each country, the population subject to analysis was limited to students who speak the more common national language at home (Azerbaijani, Kazakh, Romanian and Ukrainian). Students' socio-economic background, and the socio-economic status of the schools they attend, was also accounted for. Results show that students in Kazakhstan and Moldova who speak Kazakh and Romanian, respectively, who attend Russian-speaking schools perform better than those who attend Kazakh- and Romanian-speaking schools.

Figure 1.12. Language of instruction and reading performance

Difference in reading between students who attend school in Russian and students who attend school in Azerbaijani, Kazakh, Romanian or Ukrainian (Russian minus other language)

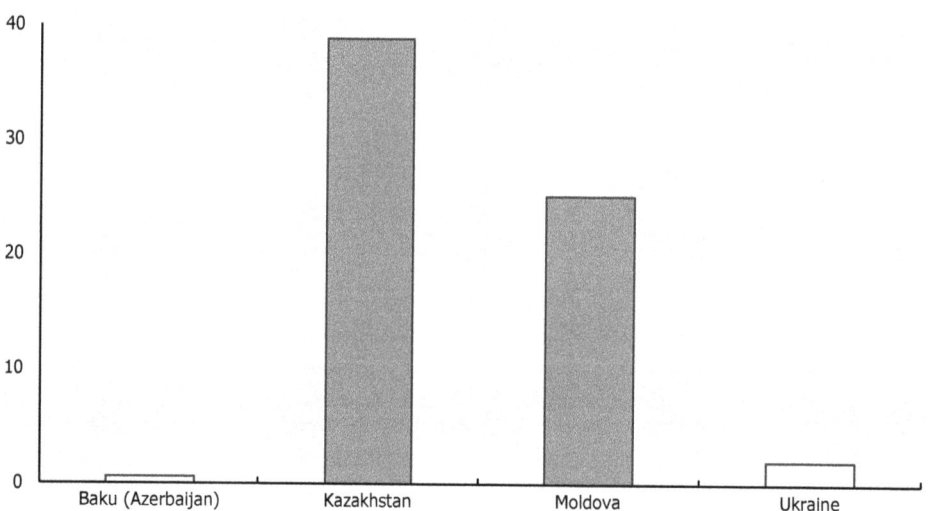

Note: Results that are statistically significant are shaded.
Source: (OECD, 2019[5]), *PISA 2018 Database*, https://www.oecd.org/pisa/data/2018database/ (accessed 17 November 2020).

StatLink https://stat.link/shbi7g

These findings suggest that school-level factors related to the language of instruction could affect student performance in Kazakhstan and Moldova (e.g. textbooks). Nevertheless, the findings should be interpreted carefully. While language spoken at home and socio-economic background are important factors, they do not represent completely all the differences between Kazakh/Romanian- and Russian-speaking populations in Kazakhstan and Moldova. It is possible that unaccounted for contextual variables (e.g. parental background) can help explain these differences.

References

Echazarra, A. and T. Radinger (2019), "Learning in rural schools: Insights from PISA, TALIS and the literature", *OECD Education Working Papers*, No. 196, OECD Publishing, Paris, https://dx.doi.org/10.1787/8b1a5cb9-en. [7]

EU (2020), *Partnership for Good Governance*, https://pjp-eu.coe.int/en/web/pgg2/home (accessed on 16 March 2021). [3]

OECD (2019), *PISA 2018 Results (Volume I): What Students Know and Can Do*, PISA, OECD Publishing, Paris, https://dx.doi.org/10.1787/5f07c754-en. [5]

OECD (2019), *PISA 2018 Results (Volume II): Where All Students Can Succeed*, PISA, OECD Publishing, Paris, https://dx.doi.org/10.1787/b5fd1b8f-en. [9]

The World Bank (n.d.), *GDP per capita (current US$) | Data*, https://data.worldbank.org/indicator/NY.GDP.PCAP.CD?locations=XK-AL-ME-MK-RS&view=chart (accessed on 1 February 2019). [6]

UNESCO-UIS (2021), *UIS dataset*, http://data.uis.unesco.org/ (accessed on 4 July 2018). [8]

UNICEF (2017), *Improving Education Participation: Policy and Practice Pointers for Enrolling All Children and Adolescents in School and Preventing Dropout*, https://www.unicef.org/eca/media/2971/file/Improving_education_participation_report.pdf (accessed on 17 December 2020). [4]

World Bank (2021), *GDP Per Capita, PPP*, https://data.worldbank.org/indicator/NY.GDP.PCAP.PP.CD (accessed on 11 January 2020). [1]

World Bank (2021), *Gini index (World Bank estimate)*, https://data.worldbank.org/indicator/SI.POV.GINI? (accessed on 16 March 2021). [2]

Notes

[1] This report focuses on PISA-participating countries in Eastern Europe and Central Asia that are supported by the UNICEF ECARO office. The ten countries from this region that participated in PISA 2018 are Azerbaijan (only the city of Baku participated in PISA 2018), Belarus, Bulgaria, Croatia, Georgia, Kazakhstan, Moldova, Romania, Turkey and Ukraine.

[2] PISA scores do not have a substantive meaning but are set in relation to the variation in results observed across all test participants. The results are scaled to fit approximately normal distributions, with means around 500 score points and standard deviations around 100 score points. The metric for each scale was set when it was first developed as a major domain. The mean reading score for the 28 OECD member countries at the time was set at 500 score points, with a standard deviation of 100 points, in PISA 2000; the OECD mean mathematics score was set at 500 in PISA 2003; and the OECD mean science score was set at 500 in PISA 2006.

[3] PISA measures a student's socio-economic status through responses on the student questionnaire in three areas—parents' level of education, parents' employment and household possessions.

2 Providing excellent and equitable schooling

Introduction

Schools are the fundamental institution of education systems. Access to high-quality schooling can equip students with the knowledge and skills they need to participate in the labour market and engage in a lifetime of learning. Quality schooling also contributes to achieving broader societal goals, such as economic development, civic participation and social cohesion. In the past decade, Eastern European and Central Asian (EECA) countries have enacted important policies to improve school practices and outcomes. These efforts include the development of modern school evaluation systems and a strong emphasis on improving the technology and connectivity of schools.

Nevertheless, data from the OECD Programme for International Student Assessment (PISA) and United Nations Children's Fund (UNICEF)-OECD country reviews show that significant challenges remain. An important overarching issue is that school quality in the region is unequal and inequitable. Especially at the upper secondary level, students in some EECA countries are segregated according to their performance, which is closely associated with their socio-economic backgrounds. Disadvantaged students, therefore, tend to be concentrated in certain schools, often according to geography or programme type. School resourcing policies risk exacerbating, rather than mitigating, these disparities. Overall spending in the education sector is low compared to international benchmarks, and available resources are not always allocated to where they are needed most. At the same time, students in the region, particularly the most vulnerable, generally receive less in-class learning time and are more likely to be truant, which can further worsen inequalities.

This chapter uses PISA data to analyse school policies in EECA countries, with a focus on school sorting and segregation, school resourcing, learning time and truancy. This analysis can inform the efforts of EECA countries to develop better school policies that supports the learning of all students.

Student sorting and segregation

Similar to many OECD countries, most EECA countries sort students into different pathways and programmes at the upper secondary level. However, what distinguishes student grouping in the EECA region is the high levels of academic selectivity of schools, and the resulting segregation between high- and low-achieving students in some countries, which frequently occurs along socio-economic lines. These practices contribute to an achievement gap between students who attend elite schools that often act as gateways to the best universities and jobs, and students who attend less prestigious schools that might offer more limited opportunities. PISA data highlight the need for more deliberate policy efforts to improve school quality for disadvantaged students, not just once they reach upper secondary school but above all in the formative early years.

Data from PISA

Student grouping in upper secondary schools is largely based upon academic criteria

As mentioned in Chapter 1, student grouping in upper secondary school in EECA countries is often more complicated than simply tracking into general and vocational pathways. In many countries, upper secondary schools have a certain academic profile, meaning they focus more intently on a certain discipline. In Turkey, students can attend up to seven different types of upper secondary schools. Students are often selected into their programmes on the basis of their academic credentials, which include results on high-stakes examinations.

PISA 2018 data show that EECA countries, compared to OECD countries, are generally more academically selective when allocating students to upper secondary schools. On average 61% of students in EECA countries attend an upper secondary school where a student's record of academic performance is always considered for school admission, compared to 45% across the OECD (Table 2.1). However, this average conceals wide disparities within the region. In Bulgaria, Croatia, Romania and Turkey, over 80% of students in upper secondary school are selected based upon their academic performance, which are some of the highest rates across all PISA-participating countries. At the same time, in Georgia and Ukraine less than 40% of students attend schools where academic performance is considered for school admission.

Table 2.1. Criteria for admission into upper secondary education

Percentage of students whose principals indicated that students are selected into their schools based on:

	Student's record of academic performance	Residence in a particular area
Baku (Azerbaijan)	59	65
Belarus	41	45
Bulgaria	81	16
Croatia	90	5
Georgia	28	22
Kazakhstan	54	52
Romania	82	8
Turkey	80	13
Ukraine	37	48
EECA average - 9	61	31
OECD average	45	32

Notes: Moldova is not included in the table since most students in the country are in lower secondary education, where selection based on performance is generally less prevalent.
Darker tones indicate greater academic selectivity and less selectivity based upon place of residence.
The data for this table were collected before Costa Rica became an OECD member.
Source: (OECD, 2019[1]), *PISA 2018 Database*, https://www.oecd.org/pisa/data/2018database/ (accessed 17 November 2020).

StatLink https://stat.link/no4wzg

Students can be highly segregated in terms of performance and background

Numerous OECD reviews have noted that a disproportionate share of students in some EECA countries apply to enter the upper secondary schools that are widely regarded as the most elite. In addition to having the highest achieving student intakes, these schools are often equipped with the latest technology and have the most qualified staff (Kitchen et al., 2019[2]; OECD, 2017[3]). Examples include Anatolian schools in Turkey and mathematics and foreign language schools in Bulgaria. While such grouping can help identify and nurture the top performing students, it can also isolate students from each other and reinforce inequalities based on factors such as socio-economic status.

PISA 2018 created "isolation indices", which measure the likelihood that students from the same group attend the same school. High isolation indices, on a scale of zero to one, indicate that students from the same group are likely to attend the same school (OECD, 2020[4]). According to this measure, students in some EECA countries are more clustered on the basis of their academic performance than students in other PISA-participating countries (Figure 2.1). This trend is particularly pronounced in Turkey and Bulgaria, where high-achieving students are the most isolated among all PISA-participating counties, and low-achieving students are among the most isolated. On the other hand, Baku (Azerbaijan) exhibits some of the lowest levels of isolation among PISA-participating countries.

In general, high-achieving and low-achieving students in EECA countries are equally isolated, which suggests that all students undergo similar academic selection procedures. The exceptions are students in Moldova and Kazakhstan. High-achieving students in these countries are more likely than low-achieving students to be grouped together, which suggests the presence of a small number of elite, selective schools, such as the Nazarbayev Intellectual Schools in Kazakhstan.

Figure 2.1. The likelihood that low- and high-achieving students attend the same school

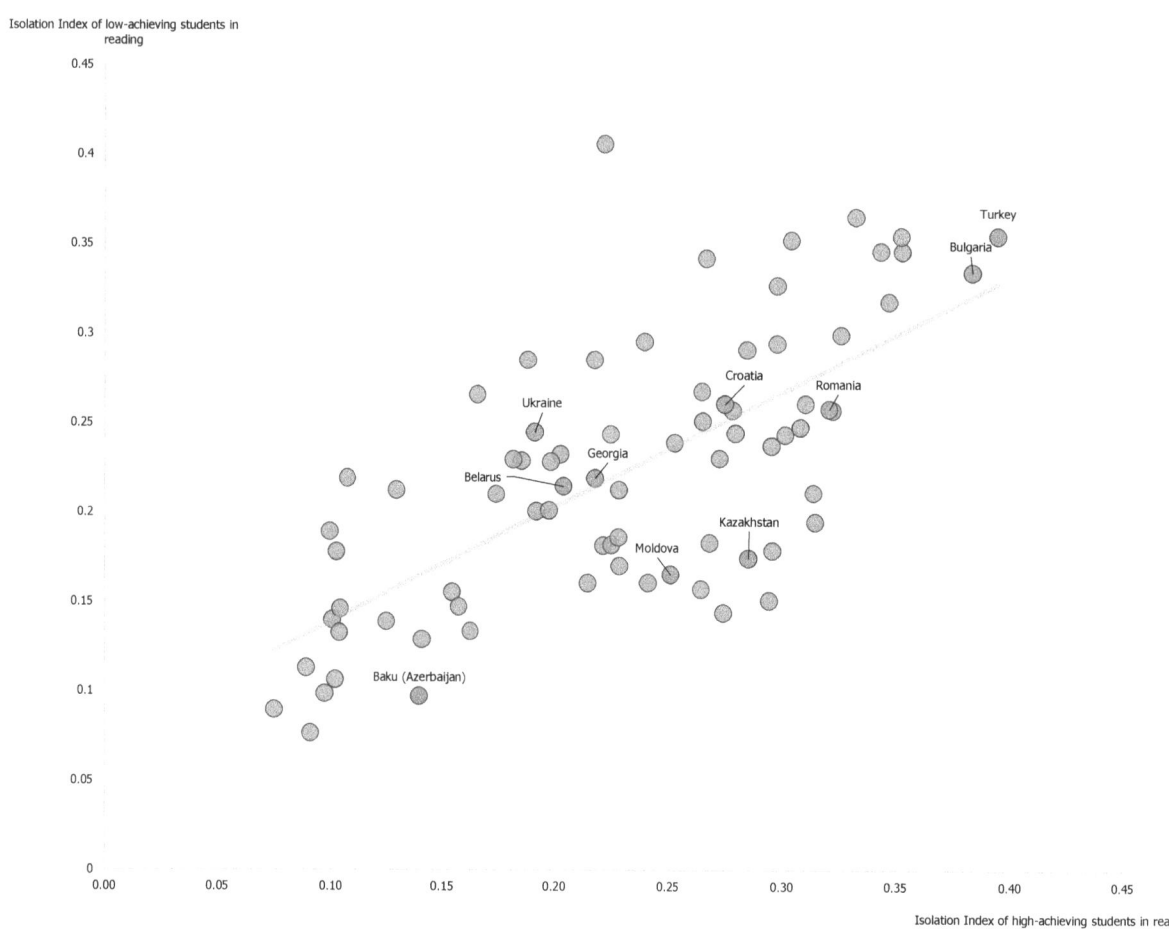

Note: EECA economies are marked and labelled in red.
Source: (OECD, 2019[1]), *PISA 2018 Database*, Tables II.B1.4.2 and II.B1.4.3, https://www.oecd.org/pisa/data/2018database/ (accessed 17 November 2020).

StatLink https://stat.link/jgf73s

In countries where academic performance is strongly correlated with socio-economic status, student selection can be closely related with student background, which can negatively affect equity. The OECD created another isolation index to measure the likelihood that socio-economically disadvantaged students are enrolled in the same school as a high-achieving student. Six out of ten EECA countries have an isolation index in this area higher than the OECD average. Socio-economically disadvantaged students in Belarus, Bulgaria and Romania are some of the least likely among similar students in PISA-participating countries to be enrolled in the same school as high-achieving students (OECD, 2019[1]). These results suggest that students in these three countries might be grouped based partly on socio-economic background rather than strictly academic achievement. Meanwhile, Baku (Azerbaijan) and Kazakhstan demonstrate comparatively low levels of isolation between socio-economically disadvantaged students and high-achieving students.

Policy implications

Improve the quality of education in lower levels of schooling

Gaps in the educational achievement of 15-year-olds are reflective of the unequal learning opportunities they had in lower levels of schooling. The sources of these inequalities are diverse and require diverse responses to address. In the context of EECA countries, where there is a strong emphasis on academic competition and identifying elite students, an important issue is perceptions towards students who are not necessarily the highest performers. Schools and teachers need to develop attitudes and practices (and be supported in doing so) that help each student achieve their full potential (see Chapter 3).

A critical concern for education in the region is the unbalanced distribution of educational resources across schools. There are large disparities in terms of their materials, learning time and who students' peers are, which contribute to different levels of achievement and unfair sorting into upper secondary schools. Other sections of this report examine these issues and discuss policy measures that countries can consider in order to improve the outcomes and outlooks of all students.

Ensure that all academic programmes are authentic and valuable

The most important consideration when grouping students into different programmes is ensuring that all options are authentic and valuable (OECD, 2017[5]). Vocational pathways in particular, which tend to enrol a disproportionately high share of lower-achieving and disadvantaged students, can sometimes have more limited opportunities for further education and entry into the labour market. Students who are sorted into less attractive and/or suitable pathways are at greater risk of dropping out, not pursuing further education or training and being unemployed (OECD, 2020[6]; OECD, 2017[5]).

In many EECA countries there is considerable attention given to, and pressure to attend, the most elite schools. Nevertheless, most students do not enrol in prestigious schools, and it is critical that governments in the region make sure that all programmes support students to succeed. Several countries in the region have taken measures to improve the value of all upper secondary programmes, particularly in vocational pathways. In 2005, Romania implemented a comprehensive National Qualifications Framework (NQF) that recognises specific vocational qualifications, which helps vocational students find suitable employment (Musset, 2014[7]). Allowing greater flexibility can also help ensure the value of all pathways. For example, Croatia developed a national vocational curriculum in 2018 that also allows for 30% of student time to be spent flexibly on elective modules (CEDEFOP, 2020[8]), which enables students acquire additional skills and prevents from being trapped along their trajectories.

Reforming selection instruments and criteria can help make student sorting more equitable

A critical issue when sorting students is how to fairly select students into their respective groups. In many EECA countries, selection is strongly based on academic considerations. Since education in lower levels of education is inequitable, selection into upper secondary schools based on academic criteria can reflect those inequities.

Countries in the region are enacting several measures to improve the fairness and equity of student selection. One set of measures is related to the selection tools. Many EECA countries rely heavily on examinations to select students, which has the potential of creating a fairer process (OECD, 2013[9]). However, UNICEF-OECD reviews have found that these examinations typically assess large amounts of detailed knowledge, which, when considering the relatively lower levels of in-class learning time, can contribute to students seeking out inequitable, private educational opportunities (see section on Learning time). Bulgaria and Turkey are in the process of improving the alignment of their examinations with newly introduced curricula so they assess a wider variety of skills instead of a narrower set of facts (Kitchen et al.,

2019[2]). These measures can help discourage students from participating in commercial tutoring, as they are better able to prepare for the examinations through regular classroom instruction.

Another set of measures is related to reducing the emphasis on academic criteria, which can help create a fairer process for students who did not receive equal educational opportunities in lower levels of schooling. For example, Turkey has recently added students' rates of attendance and the enrolment of family members as selection criteria for upper secondary school (Kitchen et al., 2019[2]).

School resourcing

On average across EECA countries, education spending as a percentage of national gross domestic product (GDP) is less than that of OECD countries (Table 2.2). As a result, education systems in the region face a range of resource concerns from facilities in need of major repairs to inadequate technological infrastructure (Li et al., 2019[10]; OECD, 2020[11]). Within this context, it is even more important for education systems to allocate resources in ways that best support high-quality teaching and learning for all students.

Table 2.2. Education system funding

Country	Education funding (all levels) as percentage of GDP (year)
Azerbaijan	2.5 (2018)
Belarus	4.8 (2017)
Bulgaria	4.1 (2017)
Croatia	3.9 (2017)
Georgia	3.5 (2018)
Kazakhstan	2.6 (2018)
Moldova	5.4 (2018)
Romania	3.1 (2017)
Turkey	4.7 (2017)
Ukraine	5.4 (2017)
EECA average	3.9%
OECD average	5.4%

Notes: Reference year for Canada is 2011 and for Korea 2016 (in OECD average).
The data for this table were collected before Costa Rica became an OECD member.
Sources: (UNESCO-UIS, 2018[12])*Government expenditure on education as a percentage of GDP*, http://data.uis.unesco.org/ (accessed 7 December 2020); except for Greece and Turkey, International Monetary Fund, *Government Finance Statistics, Expenditure by Functions of Government*, https://data.imf.org/ (accessed 7 December 2020): and Canada, World Bank, *World Bank Open Data, Government expenditure on education*, (https://data.worldbank.org/ (accessed 7 December 2020).

Data from PISA

Overall educational resourcing is lower in the EECA region

PISA 2018 data show that overall educational spending in EECA countries is considerably below the OECD average, and that there is a relationship between spending and student achievement. Nevertheless, some countries perform higher than would be expected from their expenditure levels, such as Belarus, Croatia, Turkey and Ukraine (Figure 2.2.). These results suggest that how resources are allocated and used, in addition to how much is provided, can significantly shape how well students learn.

Figure 2.2. Spending on education and average reading performance

Notes: Data for Baku (Azerbaijan) and Georgia are not available. The data for this table were collected before Costa Rica became an OECD member.
Source: (OECD, 2019[1]), *PISA 2018 Database*, Tables I.B1.4 and B3.1.1, https://www.oecd.org/pisa/data/2018database/ (accessed 17 November 2020).

To better understand school resourcing, PISA 2018 asked school principals to indicate whether a shortage or inadequacy of key educational resources hindered instruction at their schools. These key resources are defined here as:

- physical infrastructure (e.g. school buildings, heating and cooling systems, and instructional space)
- educational materials (e.g. textbooks, laboratory equipment, instructional material and computers)
- human resources (i.e. teachers and teaching assistants).

Table 2.3 shows how principals in EECA countries responded to questions about these resources compared to principals from other countries. On average, principals in EECA countries are about as likely as principals across the OECD to report that a shortage of material resources (defined by PISA as both physical infrastructure and educational materials) hinders instruction. There is, however, considerable variation across countries. Principals in Baku (Azerbaijan), Croatia, Georgia and Kazakhstan were more likely to report that shortages in or inadequacy of physical infrastructure hinder instruction. In Ukraine principals were more likely to report that a lack of educational materials hinders instruction.

In terms of human resources, there is little variation across EECA countries and overall levels of concern are similar to the OECD average. This finding is consistent with other PISA data showing relatively high levels of certified teachers and those with Master's degrees (proxies for teacher quality, see Chapter 3). Nevertheless, other evidence suggests that teachers' qualifications might not signal that they use modern practices that can help all students learn. There are also noticeable disparities in instructional practices among different types of schools, highlighting a need for policies to go beyond focusing on teacher certification and qualification levels to more closely examine differences in teaching practices. Chapter 3 reviews these issues in greater detail.

Table 2.3. Principal's perception of key educational resources

Percentage of students in schools whose principal reported that the school's capacity to provide instruction was hindered a lot by the following:

	Material resources				Human resources			
	A lack of educational material	Inadequate or poor quality educational material	A lack of physical infrastructure	Inadequate or poor quality physical infrastructure	A lack of teaching staff	Inadequate or poorly qualified teaching staff	A lack of assisting staff	Inadequate or poorly qualified assisting staff
Baku (Azerbaijan)	2	5	19	15	8	2	5	0
Belarus	3	1	4	6	1	1	0	1
Bulgaria	2	1	9	5	1	1	1	0
Croatia	10	11	29	28	1	1	14	1
Georgia	7	5	14	14	1	1	5	1
Kazakhstan	7	6	8	15	3	2	2	3
Moldova	5	5	5	4	3	2	3	1
Romania	8	7	6	6	0	0	3	4
Turkey	1	2	5	4	3	0	11	4
Ukraine	18	11	10	6	3	2	8	3
EECA average	6	5	11	10	2	1	5	2
OECD average	5	4	9	9	4	1	8	3

Notes: Darker shades of colour indicate greater reported lack of resources.
☐ Less than 5
☐ 5 to 10
▨ 10 to 15
▨ 15 to 20
■ Greater than 20
The data for this table were collected before Costa Rica became an OECD member.
Source: (OECD, 2019[1]), *PISA 2018 Database*, https://www.oecd.org/pisa/data/2018database/ (accessed 17 November 2020).

StatLink https://stat.link/mcjikr

An increasingly important material resource for schools is their technological infrastructure. In all EECA countries, and especially in Turkey, the computer-to-student ratio in schools is below the OECD average (Figure 2.3). In terms of the share of computers connected to the Internet, schools in the EECA region are slightly less connected than those across the OECD. Nevertheless, EECA countries have made considerable progress in providing technological infrastructure. Since 2009, Kazakhstan has increased its share of computers connected to the Internet. In 2009, roughly half of computers were connected to the Internet in Georgia and Moldova (OECD, 2010[13]). In 2018, about 96% and 81% were, respectively.

Figure 2.3. School technological infrastructure

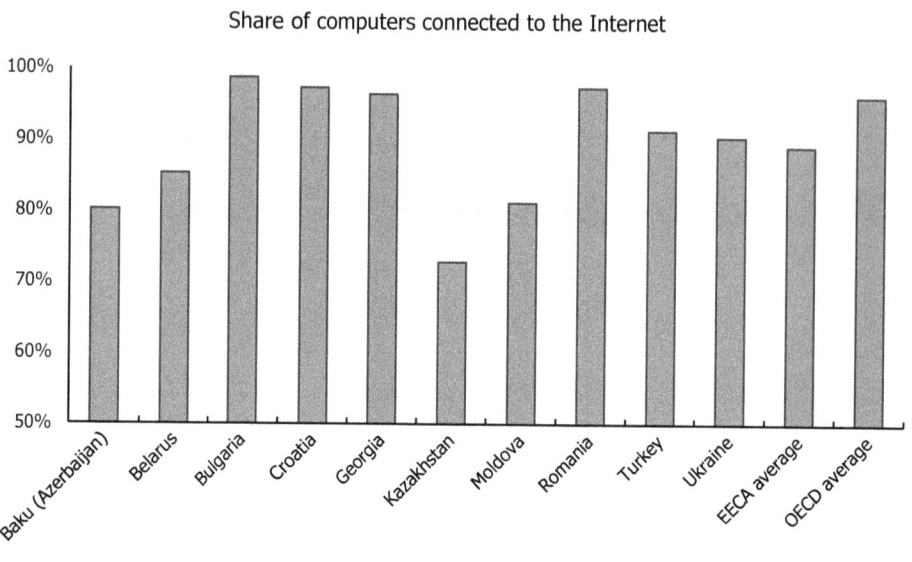

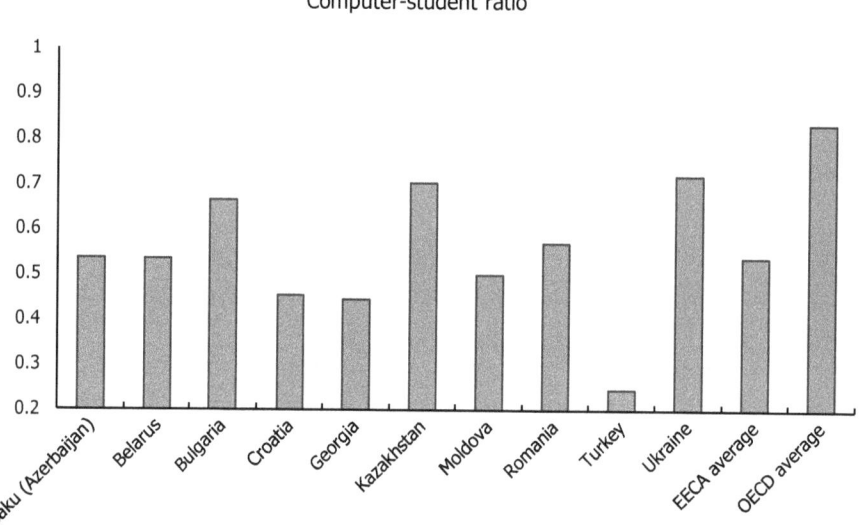

Note: The data for this figure were collected before Costa Rica became an OECD member.
Source: (OECD, 2019[1]), *PISA 2018 Database*, https://www.oecd.org/pisa/data/2018database/ (accessed 17 November 2020).

StatLink https://stat.link/qp2b3n

Principals in some EECA countries perceive their levels of technological resourcing as inadequate (Table 2.4). In Ukraine, only 25% of principals agreed that the number of digital devices for instruction is sufficient, compared to the OECD average of 59%. Roughly 22% of principals in Moldova believe that the availability of adequate software is sufficient, compared to 71% across the OECD. A larger share of principals consider teachers to have the technical and pedagogical skills to integrate digital devices in instruction.

Table 2.4. Principals' perceptions of technological infrastructure

Percentage of students in schools whose principal agreed or strongly agreed with the following statements:

	An effective online learning support platform is available	The number of digital devices for instruction is sufficient	The availability of adequate software is sufficient	Teachers have the necessary technical and pedagogical skills to integrate digital devices in instruction
Baku (Azerbaijan)		59	71	65
Belarus		58	65	86
Bulgaria		42	70	80
Croatia	49	65	58	62
Georgia	60	50	90	73
Kazakhstan	70	67	73	90
Moldova		42	22	73
Romania	51	44	44	79
Turkey	66	78	68	75
Ukraine	64	25	78	81
EECA average	49	50	59	76
OECD average	54	59	71	65

Notes: Darker tones indicate greater agreement.
☐ Less than 25
☐ 25 to 50
▨ 50 to 60
▨ 60 to 70
■ Greater than 70
The data for this table were collected before Costa Rica became an OECD member.
Source: (OECD, 2019[1]), *PISA 2018 Database*, https://www.oecd.org/pisa/data/2018database/ (accessed 17 November 2020).

StatLink ⟶ https://stat.link/jymavu

Educational resourcing in EECA countries is inequitable

In addition to the overall level of resource provision, it is important to consider whether resources are going to where they are most needed, as there is considerable evidence that students from more disadvantaged backgrounds might require comparatively greater levels of support in order to reach their potential (OECD, 2017[14]). In EECA countries, equity around school resourcing is a particularly important issue because of lower overall levels of funding and the region's tendency to isolate the top performing students into well-resourced, elite schools, which can worsen inequity.

Across OECD countries, socio-economically advantaged schools tend to be better resourced than disadvantaged schools[1] (Figure 2.4). This same trend is found in the EECA region, though there are differences across countries. Principals from socio-economically disadvantaged schools in Georgia, Kazakhstan and especially Turkey are more likely to report that shortages in material resources hinder instruction than principals who work in similar schools in other EECA countries. Similarly, principals from rural schools in EECA countries, particularly in Romania, Kazakhstan and Ukraine, are more likely than their OECD counterparts to report concerns about material resources.

Figure 2.4. Principals' perceptions of material resources, by school socio-economic status and location

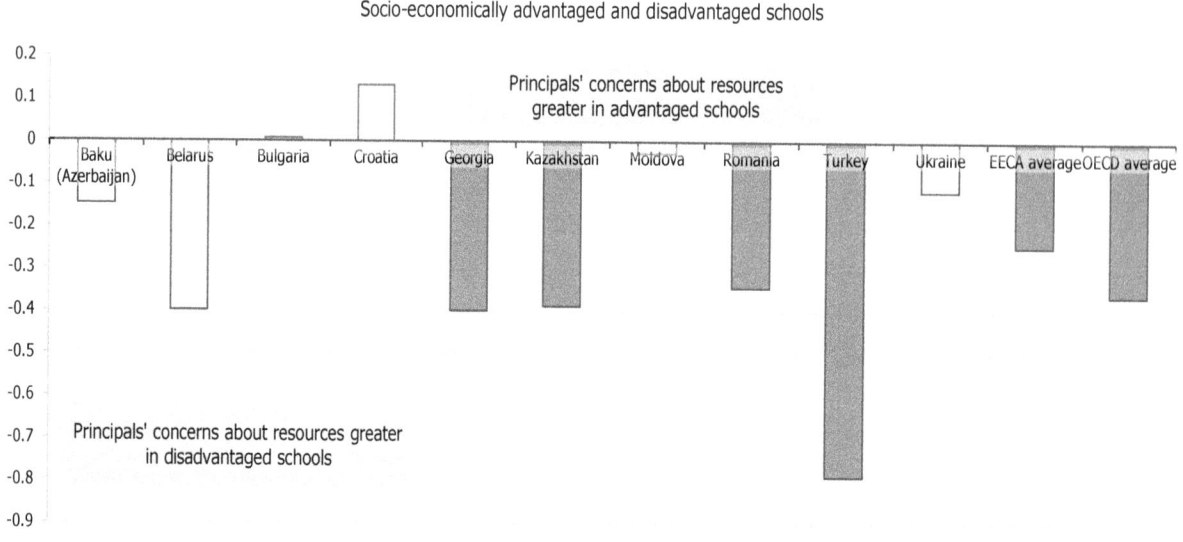

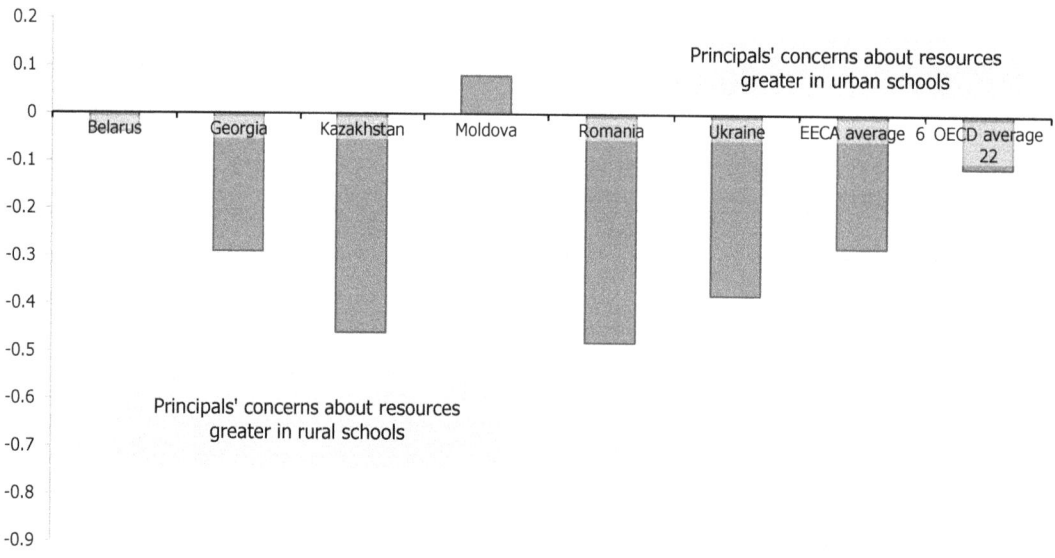

Notes: The index of material resources is calibrated such that the OECD average is zero, and a value of one represents one standard deviation away from the OECD average. The analysis is based on schools with the modal International Standard Classification of Education (ISCED) level for 15-year-old students.
Values that are statistically significant are shaded.
Missing countries on the bottom part of the figure had 3% or less of 15-year-old students enrolled in rural schools (hence "EECA average 6" and "OECD average 22").
The data for this figure were collected before Costa Rica became an OECD member.
Source: (OECD, 2019[1]), *PISA 2018 Database*, Table V.B1.4.1, Table V.B1.5.2, https://www.oecd.org/pisa/data/2018database/ (accessed 17 November 2020).

StatLink https://stat.link/e6wui8

Regarding technological resources, In Baku (Azerbaijan) and Romania, socio-economically advantaged schools have a higher number of computers per student than disadvantaged schools, while in Croatia and Moldova the opposite is true (Figure 2.5). In Georgia, urban schools have a higher number of computers per student than rural schools, while in Belarus, Kazakhstan and Moldova rural schools have more computers per student. Principals' perceptions of the adequacy of technological resources mirror these trends. Principals in socio-economically advantaged schools tend to think their technological resources are more adequate than principals from disadvantaged schools (Table 2.5).

Figure 2.5. Difference in computer-student ratio by type of school

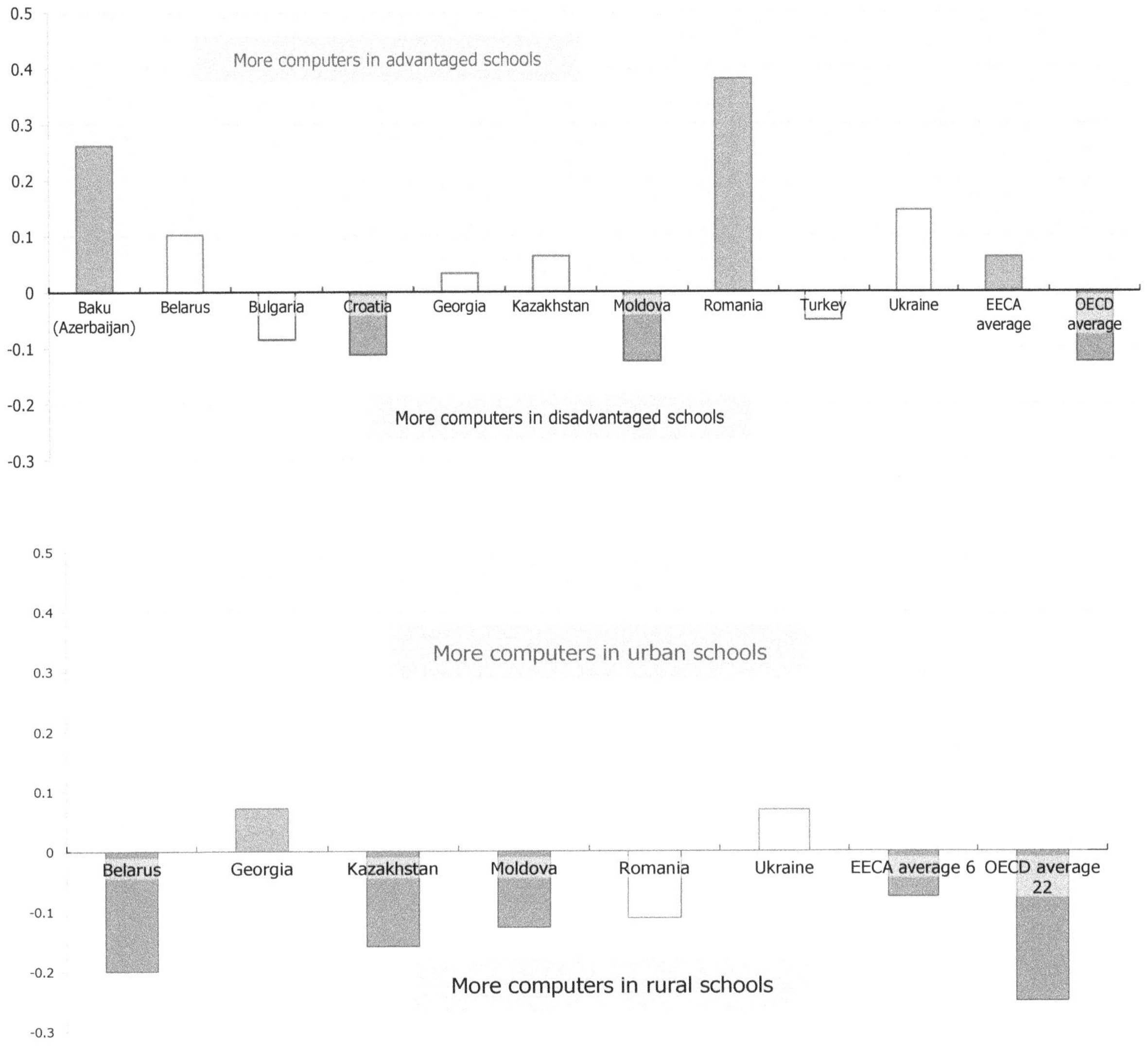

Notes: Values that are statistically significant are shaded.
Ratio of school computers available to 15-year-olds for educational purposes is to the total number of students in the modal grade for 15-year-olds, based on principals' reports.
Missing countries on the bottom part of the figure had 3% or less of 15-year-old students enrolled in rural schools (hence "EECA average 6" and "OECD average 22").
The data for this figure were collected before Costa Rica became an OECD member.
Source: (OECD, 2019[1]), *PISA 2018 Database*, Table V.B1.5.6, https://www.oecd.org/pisa/data/2018database/ (accessed 17 November 2020).

StatLink https://stat.link/25e1oj

Table 2.5. Principals' perceptions of technological infrastructure in advantaged and disadvantaged schools

Difference in the percentage of students in schools (advantaged minus disadvantaged) whose principal agreed or strongly agreed with the following statements:

	An effective online learning support platform is available	The number of digital devices for instruction is sufficient	The availability of adequate software is sufficient	Teachers have the necessary technical and pedagogical skills to integrate digital devices in instruction
Baku (Azerbaijan)	23	18	9	-2
Belarus	4	23	18	-4
Bulgaria	24	4	-2	4
Croatia	-8	-1	-3	-8
Georgia	12	25	-8	1
Kazakhstan	12	7	1	1
Moldova	-1	8	13	15
Romania	19	26	28	14
Turkey	21	28	40	14
Ukraine	5	12	0	-13
EECA average	11	15	10	2
OECD average	10	11	11	7

▨ Higher capacity in socio-economically advantaged schools
☐ Higher capacity in socio-economically disadvantaged schools
Note: The data for this table were collected before Costa Rica became an OECD member.
Source: (OECD, 2019[1]), *PISA 2018 Database*, https://www.oecd.org/pisa/data/2018database/ (accessed 17 November 2020).

StatLink ⟶ https://stat.link/pryhk8

Resource shortages, both real and perceived, are not necessarily related to student performance

While a minimum level of resources is undoubtedly necessary for instruction, providing adequate resources is not enough to ensure that students learn. Those resources also need to be relevant to schools' needs and school staff need to have the capacity to use those resources. If these conditions are not met, then more resources will not necessarily lead to better outcomes and countries risk inefficiently investing limited educational funds.

PISA 2018 shows that the relationship between resourcing and educational outcomes is not conclusive (OECD, 2020[15]). In some countries, greater resourcing (whether real or perceived) is associated with higher performance, while in others there is no relationship, or even a negative one. This trend is also found among EECA countries. With respect to computer-to-student ratios, there is a positive association with reading performance in Belarus, Kazakhstan and Ukraine, after accounting for students' and schools' socio-economic profile, but a negative one in Turkey. Kazakhstan is the only EECA country where there is a positive association between the percentage of computers connected to the Internet and reading performance. Aside from for the availability of software in Ukraine, there is no association in any country between principals' perception of technological infrastructure and student performance (Table 2.6).

Table 2.6. School resources and reading performance

Association between reading performance and the following variables

	Shortage of material resources	Number of available computers per student for educational purposes	Percentage of computers connected to the Internet	Percentage of students in schools whose principal agreed or strongly agreed that:			
				The number of digital devices for instruction is sufficient	The availability of adequate software is sufficient	Teachers have the necessary technical and pedagogical skills to integrate digital devices in instruction	An effective online learning support platform is available
Baku (Azerbaijan)							
Belarus		+					
Bulgaria							
Croatia							
Georgia							
Kazakhstan		+	+				
Moldova							
Romania							
Turkey		−					
Ukraine		+			+		
EECA average							
OECD average	−	−					

■ Positive association
□ Negative association

Notes: Results based on linear regression models, after accounting for the students' and schools' socio-economic status.
The data for this table were collected before Costa Rica became an OECD member.
Source: (OECD, 2019[1]), *PISA 2018 Database*, https://www.oecd.org/pisa/data/2018database/ (accessed 17 November 2020).

Policy implications

Adequate funding policies can enable more equitable allocations of educational resources

To direct resources to where they are most needed (and demonstrate the need for greater overall resourcing), many OECD countries use mechanisms that consider schools' student intakes. These mechanisms often include providing additional funding to specific schools (e.g. by including weights based upon student characteristics in a funding formula) or through targeted programmes (e.g. grants), which are provided for specific purposes but are separate from main allocations (OECD, 2017[14]).

Countries in the region have taken several steps to more equitably distribute resources to schools. In Romania, school funding was historically based upon the number of staff in the school. In 2010, the government switched to a per-student model with adjustments for, among several other criteria, the location of the school (i.e. rural and urban environments) (Kitchen et al., 2017[16]). Bulgaria has created a school funding formula that includes a "regional coefficient" to account for the different demographic characteristics of the country. Schools also receive additional, targeted grants from municipalities (forthcoming review). In Georgia, schools whose costs are not fully covered by other funding (the main source is student vouchers) can apply for grants from the government (Li et al., 2019[10]). While further progress can still be made, such as considering the share of highly vulnerable, ethnic minority students in funding formulae, these types of policies can nevertheless help EECA countries distribute their limited resources more efficiently.

Developing school leadership can help schools use their resources more effectively

Equally important to providing adequate resources is developing the school-level capacity needed to use those resources to help students learn. Central in this effort are school leaders, who are responsible for directing teaching and learning at their schools and deciding how resources are used (Pont, Nusche and Moorman, 2008[17]). In the EECA region, school leadership can be diverse in composition and responsibilities. In addition to the school principal, many countries have lead teachers and pedagogical councils to help manage schools (see Chapter 3 for a discussion on the autonomy that school leaders have in hiring teachers). In Kazakhstan and Romania, school leaders in larger, better resourced schools work with (or sometimes manage directly) smaller, satellite schools (OECD/The World Bank, 2015[18]; Kitchen et al., 2017[16]). Despite the importance of these roles, however, UNICEF-OECD country reviews indicate that school leaders in the region sometimes view their positions as administrative rather than instructive, and that teaching staff with leadership roles are not always certain of what their extra responsibilities are or how to perform them well (OECD, 2020[19]; Kitchen et al., 2017[16]; Li et al., 2019[10]).

Many EECA countries have taken measures to strengthen the capacity of school leaders. In 2013, Azerbaijan introduced principal standards, with a focus on shifting the role of principal away from administrator and towards an instructional leader (Kazimzade, 2017[20]). Additionally, Azerbaijan expanded the potential providers of principal training to include higher education and private institutions, which is helping improve the availability and relevance of principal professional development (ibid). Many countries in the region have introduced modern teacher standards (see Chapter 3), which spell out different levels of teachers (e.g. beginner and advanced) and their respective responsibilities, such as deciding what resources to use and helping other teachers use them. Furthermore, governments can use these standards and different levels of teachers to establish different remuneration structures, which can encourage teachers to develop their leadership capacities (OECD, 2019[21]).

Strengthening school evaluation can improve the allocation of school resources and help school leaders use their resources more effectively

Ensuring effective resourcing requires accurately identifying the needs of schools and providing adequate support so schools can use their resources to help students learn. In this regard, school evaluation frameworks are crucial because they produce data about schools that can help direct limited resources. Furthermore, the results generated by school evaluations can help school leaders understand how to use their resources to support student learning.

In EECA countries, school evaluation has historically been characterised as a compliance-oriented and somewhat high-stakes exercise (referred to in some contexts as "control"). Inspectors from a regional or central inspectorate would visit schools and evaluate them based upon how well they adhered to regulations and, if necessary, issue sanctions. The process was often disconnected from how well schools helped students learn, meaning resources were not allocated based on this consideration, and its punitive nature sometimes made schools hesitant to interact with the inspectorate and receive their support (OECD, 2020[11]; Kitchen et al., 2017[16]).

Several countries in the region have developed modern school evaluation frameworks to make school evaluation more focused on student learning and more formative. Kazakhstan, for example, is planning to reform the role of its central Committee for Control. It has proposed, but not implemented, a comprehensive framework called "school review" that bases evaluation on, among other factors, classroom observations and stakeholder interviews (OECD, 2020[11]). The results of these evaluations are intended to help the government give the tailored support that schools need to help their students learn. Bulgaria created a high-capacity National Inspectorate of Education to implement a national school inspection framework. The framework, created in 2016, evaluates schools along two broad dimensions – the educational process and management of the institution (forthcoming review). Importantly, the framework clearly sets out criteria for inclusion and equity. Based on the information generated from these evaluations, the government, often through local education bodies, can then provide necessary resources to schools and help those schools' leaders use those resources to improve the services they provide.

Learning time

The relationship between learning time and academic achievement is complex. While sufficient learning time is a key component to achieving good, and potentially more equitable, student learning outcomes, equally important is how that learning time is used (Gromada and Shewbridge, 2016[22]). Research shows that additional learning time can be more beneficial where classrooms are better managed, particularly for vulnerable student populations (Rivkin and Schiman, 2015[23]; Wu, 2020[24]). On the other hand, where learning time is insufficient or ineffectively spent, a shadow education sector can emerge to supplement formal schooling, which can exacerbate socio-economic inequities (Bray, 2020[25]). This section uses PISA data to analyse learning time in EECA countries according to three dimensions:

- Learning time in school during regular school hours
- Learning opportunities in school outside of regular school hours
- Learning time outside of school

Data from PISA

Learning time during regular school hours is significantly lower in EECA countries than the OECD average

Across EECA countries, the total average time devoted to learning in schools is roughly 2 hours below the OECD average of 27.5 hours of regular lessons per week (Figure 2.6. While there is variation across countries, all countries in EECA are below the OECD average, with Moldova having one of the lowest values among all PISA-participating countries (22.8 hours per week). At the subject-level, the largest disparity is in foreign language lessons (on average 0.7 fewer hours per week, or 24% shorter, compared to the OECD average). Regional variance was also largest in foreign language lessons, with Bulgaria devoting 4.2 hours per week on average, compared to 2.2 hours in Kazakhstan.

Learning time during regular school hours does not differ widely according to the socio-economic status of students. Only in Kazakhstan and Ukraine do socio-economically advantaged students have more total learning time than their disadvantaged peers (2.1 and 2.6 hours per week, respectively). At the subject-level, there are greater disparities, particularly for foreign language studies. In all EECA countries except in Baku (Azerbaijan) and Kazakhstan, socio-economically advantaged students studied foreign languages more than disadvantaged students. This gap is noteworthy as research shows that mastery of multiple languages is associated with better educational and employment opportunities (Marconi et al., 2020[26]).

Less learning time during regular school hours can be related to several factors. Inadequate infrastructure, especially in densely populated areas, encourages some EECA countries to make frequent use of multi-shift schools, where separate groups of students attend school in one building at different times during one day. In Croatia, an estimated 35% of schools operate in at least two shifts (World Bank, 2019[27]). Over 6% of students in Kazakhstan attended triple-shift schools in 2018 (OECD, 2020[28]). In some countries, mandatory learning time is set at relatively low levels. For example, in Moldova and Ukraine, lower secondary classes are 45 minutes in length and school years roughly 35 weeks in length. Students in these countries receive over 100 fewer hours of instruction per year compared to the OECD average (OECD, 2020[6]). While these countries also have more years of compulsory education (see Chapter 1), issues such as truancy and dropout (see section on Truancy) moderate the educational value of those extra years.

Figure 2.6. Learning time during regular school hours, by subject

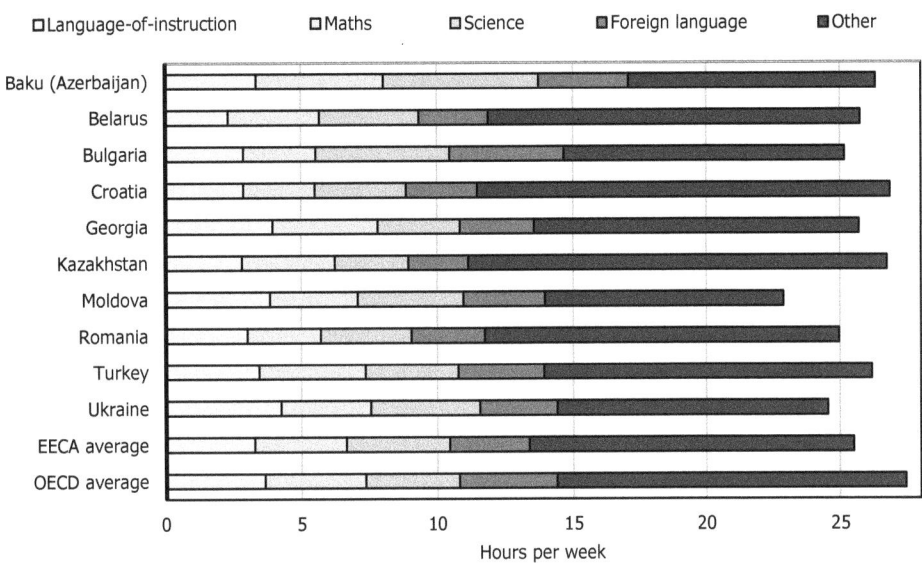

Notes: Learning time per week in regular school lessons is based on students' reports.
The data for this figure were collected before Costa Rica became an OECD member.
Source: (OECD, 2019[1]), *PISA 2018 database*, Table V.B1.6.1, Table V.B1.6.17, https://www.oecd.org/pisa/data/2018database/ (accessed 17 November 2020).

StatLink https://stat.link/fhg4wy

While ensuring that students have enough time to learn is important, PISA data show that, after a threshold of learning time is met, additional learning time might have diminishing effects on student performance. In most countries, the association between learning time during regular school hours and reading performance is positive up to 24-27 hours of instruction per week, but then declines (Figure 2.7). Data from EECA countries are consistent with international trends. This relationship could exist because governments do not always train teachers to use the additional time effectively, or because additional time is allocated to low-performing students, which can bias the overall results of students who receive a lot of learning time. These results suggest that EECA policymakers should make efforts to provide sufficient learning time, but also make efforts to ensure that additional learning time is used efficiently.

Figure 2.7. Total learning time in regular school lessons and reading performance

Learning time expressed in terms of hours per week

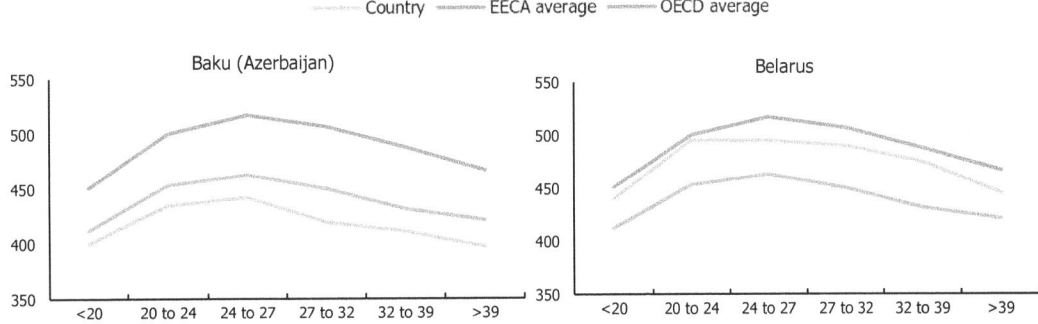

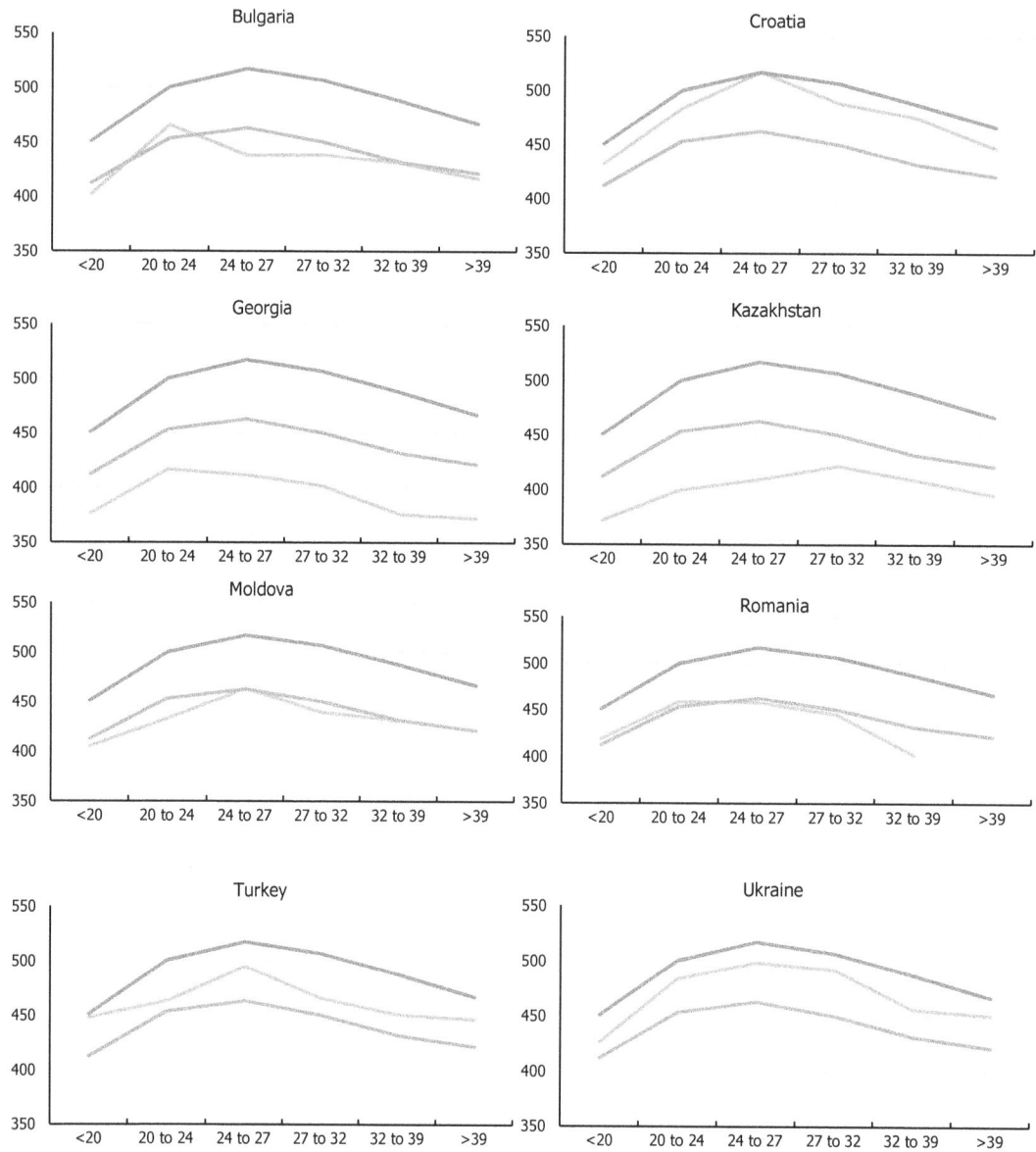

Note: The data for this figure were collected before Costa Rica became an OECD member.
Source: (OECD, 2019[1]), *PISA 2018 database*, Table V.B1.6.15, https://www.oecd.org/pisa/data/2018database/ (accessed 17 November 2020).

StatLink https://stat.link/56vuwt

Opportunities to learn outside regular school hours are relatively common, but might focus disproportionately on high-achieving students

PISA 2018 considers two types of in school learning opportunities outside of regular hours:

- After-school lessons taught by teachers
- Less formal support activities to help students study, such as peer-to-peer learning

Regarding after-school lessons, across EECA countries 68% of students attend schools that offer additional lessons in the language of instruction, compared to 46% of students in OECD countries. However, the purpose of additional lessons in EECA countries differs compared to OECD countries. EECA schools are more likely to offer enrichment lessons (10%, compared to 5% across the OECD) and much less likely to offer remedial lessons (8%, compared to 31% across the OECD) (Figure 2.8). Overall the availability of after-school lessons did not vary greatly according to students' socio-economic status; only in Bulgaria and Croatia was there a difference in the availability of such lessons (in both cases schools with more advantaged students were more likely to offer them).

Figure 2.8. Types of after-school language-of-instruction lessons offered at schools

Notes: The analysis only pertains to schools that offer after-school language-of-instruction lessons.
Values represent the percentage of students in schools where the lessons are offered.
The data for this figure were collected before Costa Rica became an OECD member.
Source: (OECD, 2019[1]), *PISA 2018 Database*, https://www.oecd.org/pisa/data/2018database/ (accessed 17 November 2020).

StatLink https://stat.link/oai9yk

Regarding other resources, EECA countries generally provide similar levels of support, but the types of activities in EECA countries differ from international benchmarks. In particular, most EECA countries seem to place stronger emphasis (relative to OECD countries) on facilitating peer-to-peer learning (i.e. students helping each other). Conversely, students in EECA countries are less likely to have access to rooms where they can do homework, though they have similar access to staff to help them (Figure 2.9). In both EECA and OECD countries, the same levels of school support are generally available to students regardless of their socio-economic background. These differences could be a reflection of the lower levels of school resourcing in EECA countries (see section on School resourcing). Providing rooms where students can do homework and staff to help them can incur greater costs in the form of rent, maintenance and salaries. However, such resources can be particularly important for students from disadvantaged families who might lack a quiet place to study or adult help at home.

Figure 2.9. Percentage of students who attend schools that provide study help outside of regular school hours

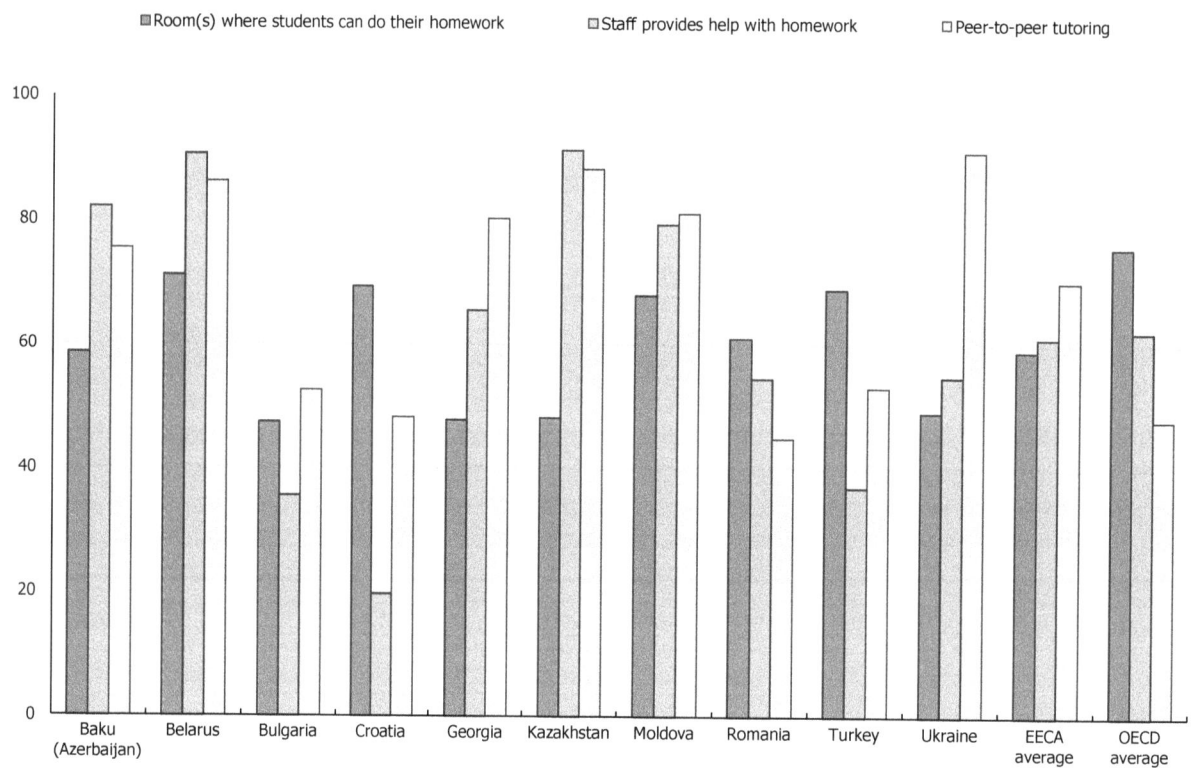

Note: The data for this figure were collected before Costa Rica became an OECD member.
Source: (OECD, 2019[1]), *PISA 2018 database*, Table V.B1.6.19, https://www.oecd.org/pisa/data/2018database/ (accessed 17 November 2020).

StatLink ᓂᕐᔅ https://stat.link/rt0ame

Learning time outside of school is higher in EECA countries

While PISA 2018 did not collect information about learning time outside of school, PISA 2012 collected this data, classified into several types of activities, from five EECA countries. These activities are:

- Doing homework or other study set by teachers
- Working with a personal tutor, whether paid or not
- Attending after-school classes organised by a commercial company, and paid for by parents
- Studying with a parent or family member

The results of PISA 2012 show that, at the time of the survey, students from some EECA countries were spending considerably more time learning outside of school than students across OECD countries (Figure 2.10). Most of this time was spent doing homework, which was also the case with students across the OECD. However, students in participating EECA countries spent comparatively more time engaged in commercial tutoring. For example, students in Kazakhstan and Turkey participated in this activity over three times as much as students across the OECD. Recent analysis by the OECD shows that governments have sought to reduce this shadow education sector, but also shows that tutoring outside school remains common in some contexts (Kitchen et al., 2019[29]; Li et al., 2019[10]; OECD, 2017[3]; OECD, 2020[28]).

The scale of learning time outside of school in the region is related to several educational, social and cultural factors. For example, high levels of learning time outside of school can signal that families are involved in the education of students. Another contributing reason could be the previously mentioned lack of learning time during regular school hours. Some teachers might not be able to progress through the curriculum in the limited time they have and perhaps assign extra homework to compensate. Students might also seek additional assistance outside of school, from tutors or parents, to help understand the material. A high-stakes sorting and examinations culture, especially in Bulgaria, Romania and Turkey (countries where grouping is more closely related with socio-economic background), might also be contributing to students seeking out learning opportunities outside of school (see Student sorting and segregation).

Figure 2.10. Learning time outside of school

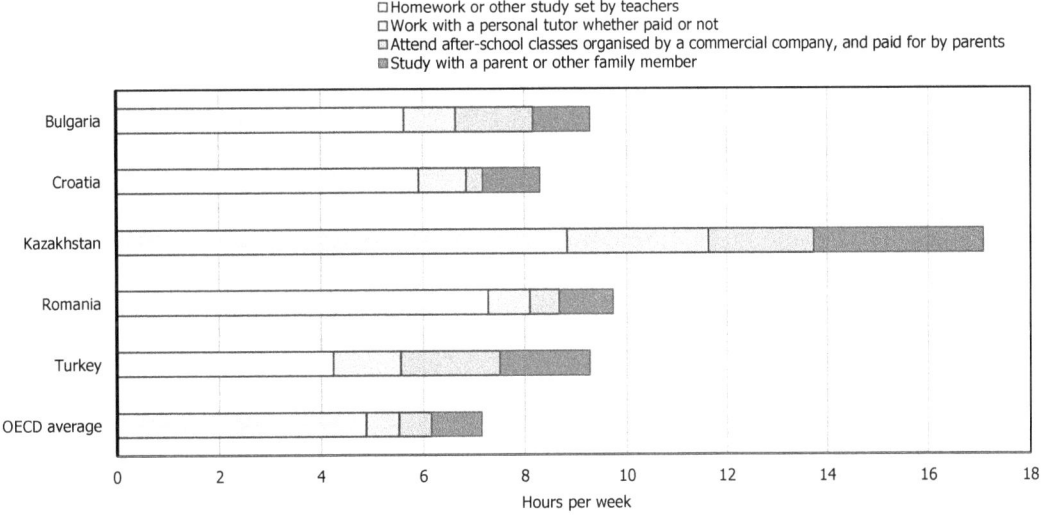

Note: The data for this figure were collected given OECD membership at the time that PISA 2012 was administered.
Source: (OECD, 2019[1]), PISA 2012 database, https://www.oecd.org/pisa/pisaproducts/pisa2012database-downloadabledata.htm (accessed 17 November 2020).

StatLink https://stat.link/gvrl0q

The amount of time that some EECA students spend learning outside of school raises concerns about equity. Since socio-economically advantaged students have more resources, they have better conditions to learn outside of school (e.g. they might have quiet spaces at home) and have greater access to different options, such as private tutoring (OECD, 2011[30]; OECD, 2013[31]). Figure 2.11 shows that, across five EECA countries that participated in PISA 2012, socio-economically advantaged students were more likely to have higher levels of outside-of-school learning time, which is likely contributing to gaps in learning outcomes.

Figure 2.11. Learning time outside of school according to socio-economic quartiles

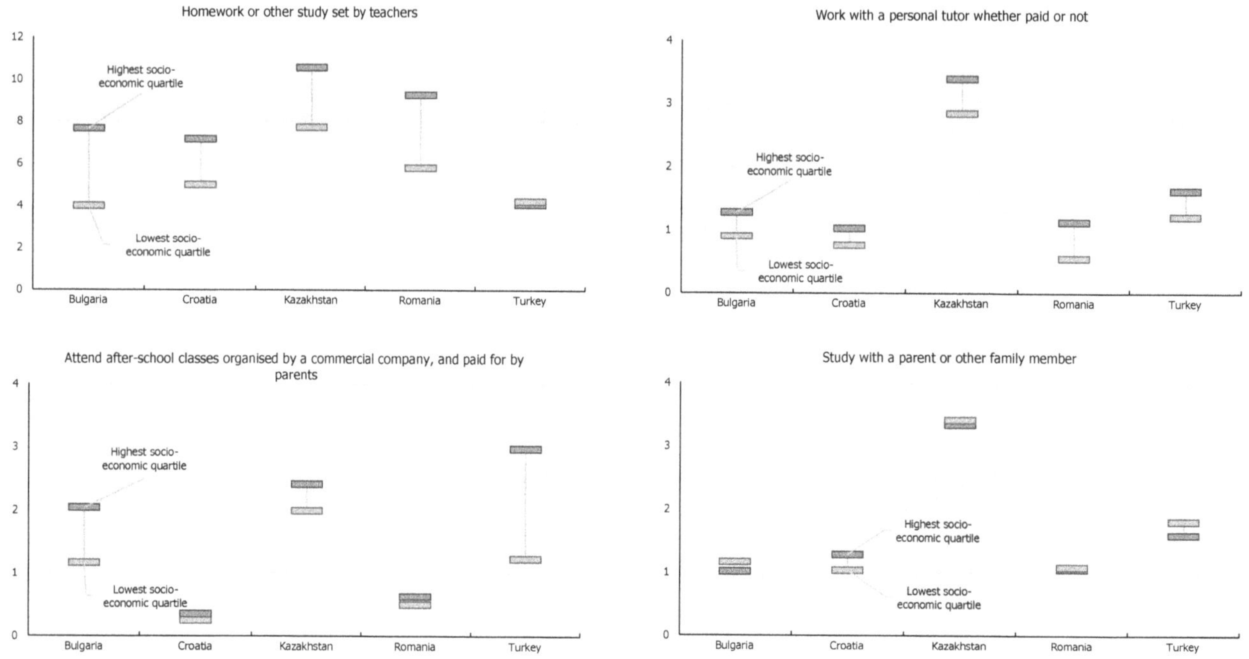

Source: (OECD, 2019[1]), *PISA 2018 Database*, https://www.oecd.org/pisa/data/2018database/ (accessed 17 November 2020).

StatLink ⟶ https://stat.link/qrxns8

Policy implications

Consider allocating more learning time during regular school hours

Ensuring sufficient learning time during school is vital to supporting student learning and equity of opportunity. Countries can alter learning time during regular school hours through addressing several aspects of schooling, including:

- The number of years of compulsory instruction
- The length of the school year
- The length of the school week
- The length of the school day, class periods, and time allocated to learning different subjects (Gromada and Shewbridge, 2016[22])

In EECA countries, the need to expand learning time during school hours is critical because current low levels might be contributing to high levels of inequitable learning time outside of school. EECA countries have made considerable efforts to extend learning time during school hours. In the past two decades all EECA countries except Belarus, Croatia and Kazakhstan have made compulsory learning longer by at least one year (World Bank, 2020[32]).

Policymakers can consider additional options to extend learning time during school hours. Kazakhstan is trying to reduce the number of multi-shift schools so schooling hours are not limited by the need to share facilities (OECD, 2020[28]). Similarly, a World Bank-funded project in Croatia aimed, among other goals, to construct new schools and reduce the number of multi-shift schools (World Bank, 2012[33]). Another option is to extend the duration of classes and/or introduce more flexible scheduling, which might make teachers and students less reliant on out-of-school learning to master the material.

Adding learning time during school hours requires considerable resources, and some research has shown that expanding instructional time can be a less efficient means of achieving learning gains than other measures, such as reducing class size (Gromada and Shewbridge, 2016[22]). Given the low levels of education spending and government revenue in the region, it is critical that any added instructional time be used effectively. Furthermore, EECA countries will need to address issues that could mitigate the effects of added learning time, such as student truancy and teacher absenteeism (see section on Truancy and Chapter 3).

Use learning opportunities outside of regular school hours to support all students

Learning outside of regular school hours is an important accompaniment to learning during school hours, but in EECA countries these opportunities, especially the most formal, structured ones, tend to target students who are doing well. Students who are struggling and already less likely to have access to high-quality learning opportunities outside of school are at risk of falling even further behind.

EECA policymakers can consider shifting the focus of out-of-school learning opportunities to help students who need the most support. Options include dedicating more school lessons to remediation and expanding the availability public resources, like rooms where students can study and community education centres. In Romania, an Anti-Poverty Package launched in 2016 established after-school remediation programmes and offered grants to schools in disadvantaged communities (OECD, 2017[34]). Turkey has created several learning centres in areas with large refugee populations to help migrant students integrate into the education system (Kitchen et al., 2019[29]).

Truancy

Student truancy is generally understood as unexcused absence from school (OECD, 2019[1]; UNICEF, 2016[35]). Preventing truancy is important because students who are truant miss valuable learning time, which affects their development and engagement, and can lead to consequences such as dropout and a greater likelihood of economic hardship and social misbehaviour, in particular crime (European Commission, 2013[36]; Campbell, 2015[37]). Research has identified student truancy as being a particular concern in the EECA region (UNICEF, 2017[38]), which heightens the need to develop effective policies to address the issue.

Data from PISA

Students in EECA countries are more likely to be truant than those in OECD countries

PISA 2018 considers a student to be truant if they have either skipped a day of school or skipped at a class in the two weeks prior to taking the PISA test. In 2018, 60% of students from EECA countries reported that they had been truant, compared to the OECD average of 33%. In Georgia, 80% reported engaging in truant behaviour, which is the highest rate of any country that participated in PISA (Korea has the lowest rate, at 3%). Only students in Croatia, the highest performing country in the region, had a lower share of truant students compared to the OECD average. These results are consistent with OECD reviews that highlighted higher levels of student dropout and irregular attendance in the region, especially among vulnerable populations such as the Roma (Kitchen et al., 2017[16]; Li et al., 2019[10]).

Figure 2.12. Percentage of students who were truant in the two weeks prior to taking PISA

Being truant is defined as having skipped school or skipped classes at least once

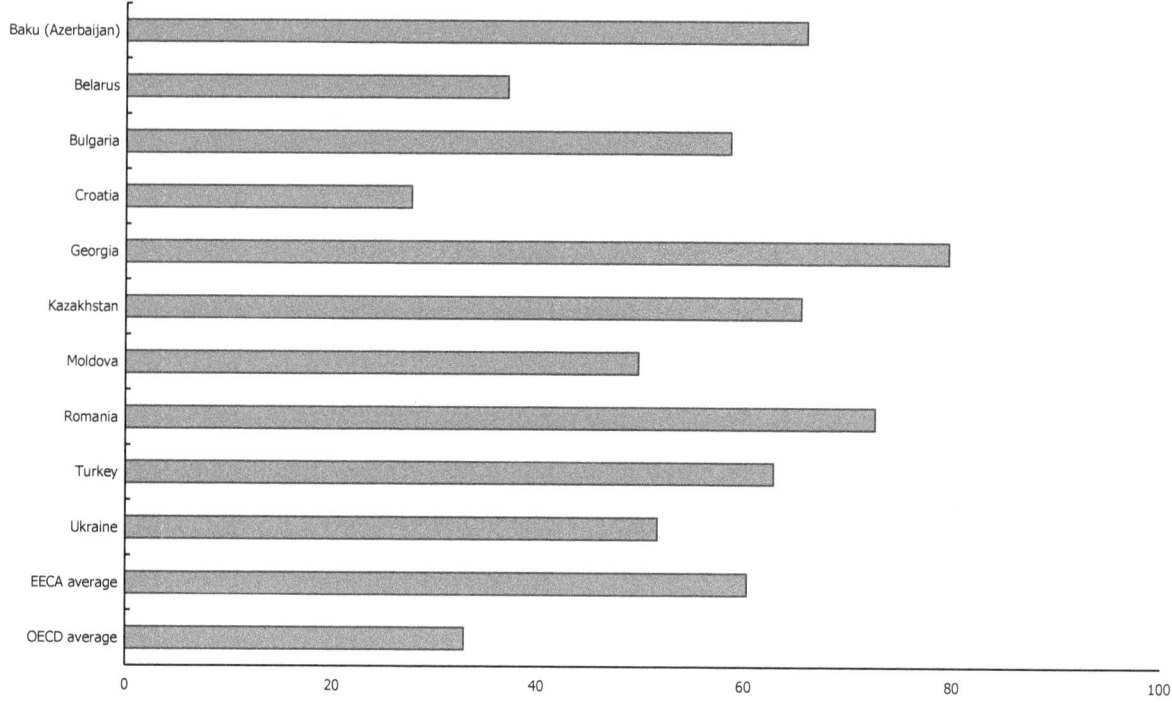

Note: The data for this figure were collected before Costa Rica became an OECD member.
Source: (OECD, 2019[1]), *PISA 2018 database*, Table III.B1.4.1, https://www.oecd.org/pisa/data/2018database/ (accessed 17 November 2020).

StatLink https://stat.link/17gciq

In general, boys and students from disadvantaged backgrounds are more likely to be truant in EECA countries, as they are across the OECD (Figure 2.13). There are significant variations across countries, however. For example, in Moldova, boys are 1.65 times more likely to be truant, and in Belarus girls are more likely to be truant. Students from disadvantaged socio-economic background in Moldova are more than twice as likely to be truant, while in Turkey socio-economically advantaged students are more likely to be truant. In no OECD country other than Turkey are socio-economically advantaged students more likely to be truant. In no EECA country with a significant share of rural students were there differences in truancy between rural and urban students.

Figure 2.13. Increased likelihood of student groups to be truant

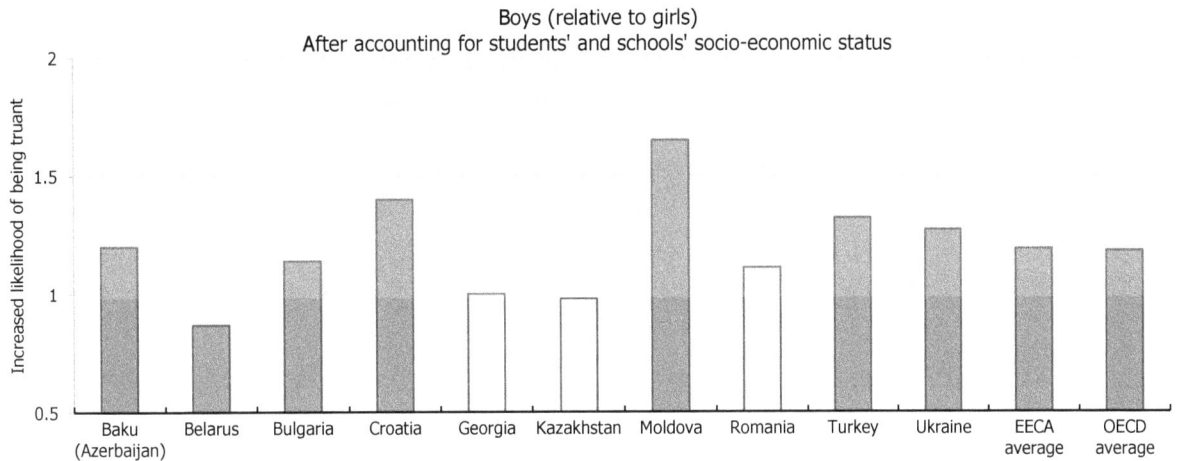

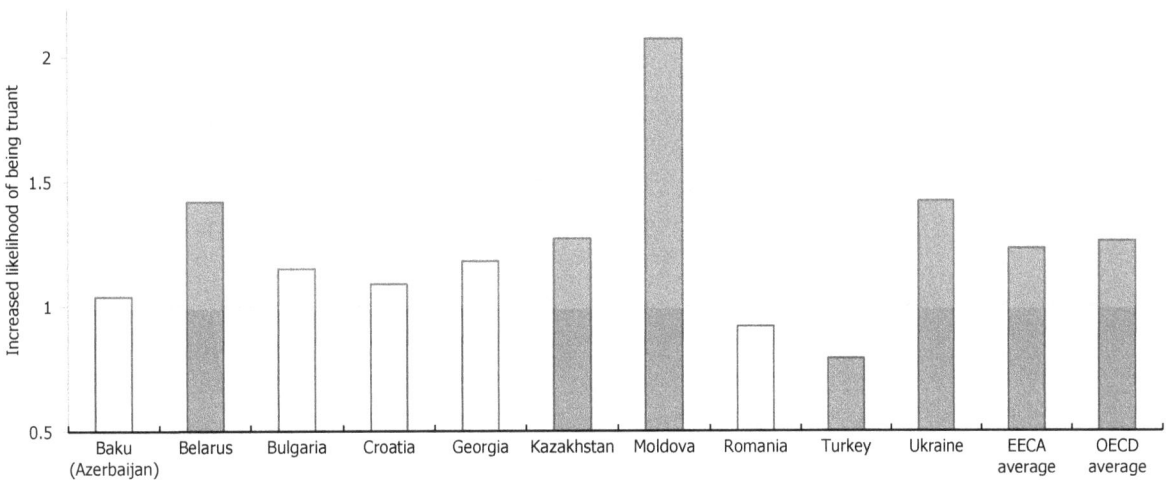

Notes: Values greater than one are considered more likely to be truant than the reference group. Values less than one are considered less likely. Values that are statistically significant are shaded.
The data for this figure were collected before Costa Rica became an OECD member.
Source: (OECD, 2019[1]), *PISA 2018 Database*, https://www.oecd.org/pisa/data/2018database/ (accessed 17 November 2020).

StatLink https://stat.link/rwlga3

Truancy in the region has a weaker association with performance

Several factors might explain why students in EECA countries demonstrate different truancy trends compared to each other and to OECD countries. One could be the lesser opportunity cost of skipping school. Given the lower levels of learning time during regular school hours in several EECA countries (see section on Learning time), many students in the region miss less instructional time by skipping school (conversely, the relative lack of value of school time might not be motivating students to miss school, but those who do simply experience less learning loss). Moreover, the share of students participating in out-of-school learning is higher in the EECA region, and some students might skip school to attend tutoring (OECD, 2017[3]; Li et al., 2019[10]).

These factors might help explain why the average difference in performance between students with the most truant tendencies (those who skipped at least three days of school in the last two weeks) and those with the least (who skipped two or fewer days) in EECA countries is less than in OECD countries (Figure 2.14). In three out of ten EECA countries, the difference in reading performance between these student groups is less than 15 score points (compared to over 55 across the OECD), and in Turkey there is no difference.

Figure 2.14. Difference in reading performance between the students with the most and least truant tendencies

Least truant minus most truant students, after accounting for gender, students' and school's socio-economic status

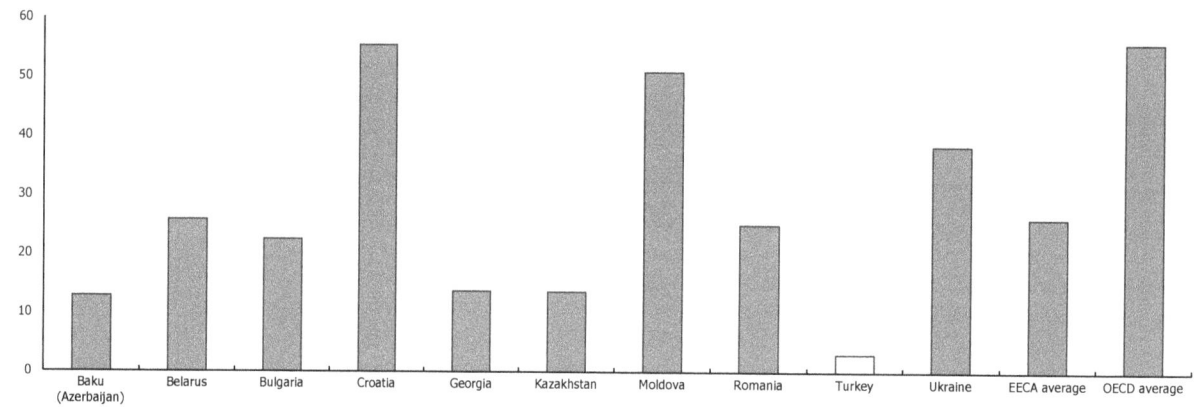

Notes: Values that are statistically significant are shaded.
The data for this figure were collected before Costa Rica became an OECD member.
Source: (OECD, 2019[1]), *PISA 2018 Database*, https://www.oecd.org/pisa/data/2018database/ (accessed 17 November 2020).

StatLink 🛲 https://stat.link/rmpfe2

Policy implications

Creating data collection and analytical tools can help identify truant students and understand truancy trends

Addressing student truancy, and avoiding further negative consequences like dropout, requires identifying which students exhibit truant behaviour, which requires developing comprehensive and integrated education data systems (UNICEF, 2016[35]). Such systems not only need to collect relevant data (e.g. when students are truant, in which schools, and the characteristics of those students), but also present the data in an accessible manner (e.g. via an analytical dashboard that can highlight at risk populations) to help inform timely policy interventions.

Georgia serves as an example of a country that has made tremendous progress in collecting relevant data and is in the process of making its data more accessible. In 2012, the Georgian Ministry of Education, Science, Culture and Sport (MoESCS) developed its national education management information system (EMIS). Georgia's EMIS holds all education data, including student attendance, and schools continuously input new data into EMIS through an internal portal called E-School (Li et al., 2019[10]). However, using the data in EMIS has sometimes been challenging. For example, principals do not have tools that allow them to view their schools' attendance rates over time or by dimensions such as gender, thus there is also no way of quickly identifying which student populations are more likely to be truant and at risk of dropping out (UNICEF, 2017[39]). In 2018, MoESCS began partnering with Microsoft to strengthen its digital ecosystem, which included the introduction of tools to help visualise and thereby analyse data in EMIS instantaneously (Microsoft, 2020[40]). These tools can help principals instantly see which students are truant, and how recent truancy data compare with previous weeks and months.

Developing warning systems and targeted programmes to address truancy

With accurate and comprehensive information management systems, countries can analyse the data they collect to develop appropriate measures to address truancy and help prevent more negative consequences like dropout (UNICEF, 2017[38]). A common approach is to develop early warning systems based upon administrative data, which can alert school staff and parents that students are exhibiting behaviours that could lead to increased truancy and dropout (EU, 2013[41]). Many countries in the European Union have implemented such systems, including Bulgaria and Croatia (ibid).

In addition to creating detection systems at the school level, EECA countries have also monitored system-level data to better understand macro trends in truancy and dropout. Based upon this information, countries have developed national initiatives to target the populations most vulnerable to being truant and dropping out. For example, the government of Bulgaria has worked closely to address persistent truancy in the country's Roma community. Efforts include organising national and local round tables to confront negative attitudes towards Roma students, and opening family centres to help prevent child marriages and promote school attendance for girls (UNICEF, 2016[42]).

Nevertheless, while such programmes can help remove obstacles to attending school, EECA countries should also consider strengthening students' intrinsic motivation (often shaped by family background) to attend school by raising the value of schooling (which might also encourage some students to attend school instead of private tutoring). To achieve this aim, policymakers can consider increasing learning time during school (see section on Learning time) and encouraging the use of more modern teaching practices (see Chapter 3).

References

Bray, M. (2020), "Shadow Education in Europe: Growing Prevalence, Underlying Forces, and Policy Implications", *ECNU Review of Education*, p. 209653111989014, http://dx.doi.org/10.1177/2096531119890142. [25]

Campbell, C. (2015), "The socioeconomic consequences of dropping out of high school: Evidence from an analysis of siblings", *Social Science Research*, Vol. 51, pp. 108-118, http://dx.doi.org/10.1016/j.ssresearch.2014.12.011. [37]

CEDEFOP (2020), *Vocational education and training in Croatia*, http://dx.doi.org/10.2801/121008. [8]

EU (2013), *Early warning systems in Europe: practice, methods and lessons*, https://ec.europa.eu/assets/eac/education/experts-groups/2011-2013/esl/europe-warning-systems_en.pdf (accessed on 25 February 2021). [41]

European Commission (2013), *Reducing early school leaving: Key messages and policy support*, https://ec.europa.eu/education/sites/education/files/early-school-leaving-group2013-report_en.pdf (accessed on 25 January 2019). [36]

Gromada, A. and C. Shewbridge (2016), "Student Learning Time: A Literature Review", *OECD Education Working Papers*, No. 127, OECD Publishing, Paris, https://dx.doi.org/10.1787/5jm409kqqkjh-en. [22]

Kazimzade, E. (2017), *School Principalship Developments in Azerbaijan: Challenges of Professional Development of School Leaders vs. Managers A case study*, http://www.edupolicy.net/wp-content/uploads/2018/03/school-principalship-developments-in-azerbaijana_eng.pdf (accessed on 8 April 2021). [20]

Kitchen, H. et al. (2019), *OECD Reviews of Evaluation and Assessment in Education: Student Assessment in Turkey*, OECD Reviews of Evaluation and Assessment in Education, OECD Publishing, Paris, https://dx.doi.org/10.1787/5edc0abe-en. [2]

Kitchen, H. et al. (2019), *OECD Reviews of Evaluation and Assessment in Education: Student Assessment in Turkey*, OECD Reviews of Evaluation and Assessment in Education, OECD Publishing, Paris, https://dx.doi.org/10.1787/5edc0abe-en. [29]

Kitchen, H. et al. (2017), *Romania 2017*, OECD Reviews of Evaluation and Assessment in Education, OECD Publishing, Paris, https://dx.doi.org/10.1787/9789264274051-en. [16]

Li, R. et al. (2019), *OECD Reviews of Evaluation and Assessment in Education: Georgia*, OECD Reviews of Evaluation and Assessment in Education, OECD Publishing, Paris, https://dx.doi.org/10.1787/94dc370e-en. [10]

Marconi, G. et al. (2020), "What matters for language learning?: The questionnaire framework for the PISA 2025 Foreign Language Assessment", *OECD Education Working Papers*, No. 234, OECD Publishing, Paris, https://dx.doi.org/10.1787/5e06e820-en. [26]

Microsoft (2020), *Microsoft Customer Story-Georgian Ministry of Education embraces the future, making digital learning a reality*, https://customers.microsoft.com/en-us/story/836788-ministry-emis-national-government-azure-en-georgia (accessed on 17 December 2020). [40]

Musset, P. (2014), *A Skills Beyond School Commentary on Romania*, OECD, https://www.oecd.org/countries/romania/ASkillsBeyondSchoolCommentaryOnRomania.pdf (accessed on 10 March 2021). [7]

OECD (2020), "Developing a school evaluation framework to drive school improvement", *OECD Education Policy Perspectives*, No. 26, OECD Publishing, Paris, https://dx.doi.org/10.1787/60b471de-en. [11]

OECD (2020), *Education at a Glance 2020: OECD Indicators*, OECD Publishing, Paris, https://dx.doi.org/10.1787/69096873-en. [6]

OECD (2020), *Education in the Western Balkans: Findings from PISA*, PISA, OECD Publishing, Paris. [15]

OECD (2020), *PISA 2018 Results (Volume V): Effective Policies, Successful Schools*, PISA, OECD Publishing, Paris, https://dx.doi.org/10.1787/ca768d40-en. [4]

OECD (2020), "Raising the quality of initial teacher education and support for early career teachers in Kazakhstan", *OECD Education Policy Perspectives*, No. 25, OECD Publishing, Paris, https://dx.doi.org/10.1787/68c45a81-en. [19]

OECD (2020), *Strengthening national examinations in Kazakhstan to achieve national goals*, https://www.oecd-ilibrary.org/education/strengthening-national-examinations-in-kazakhstan-to-achieve-national-goals_0bf8662b-en (accessed on 1 February 2021). [28]

OECD (2019), *PISA 2018 Results (Volume I): What Students Know and Can Do*, PISA, OECD Publishing, Paris, https://dx.doi.org/10.1787/5f07c754-en. [1]

OECD (2019), *Working and Learning Together: Rethinking Human Resource Policies for Schools*, OECD Reviews of School Resources, OECD Publishing, Paris, https://dx.doi.org/10.1787/b7aaf050-en. [21]

OECD (2017), *Country Reviews of Evaluation and Assessment: Romania*. [34]

OECD (2017), *Educational Opportunity for All: Overcoming Inequality throughout the Life Course*, Educational Research and Innovation, OECD Publishing, Paris, https://dx.doi.org/10.1787/9789264287457-en. [5]

OECD (2017), *OECD Reviews of Integrity in Education: Ukraine 2017*, OECD Publishing, Paris, https://dx.doi.org/10.1787/9789264270664-en. [3]

OECD (2017), *The Funding of School Education: Connecting Resources and Learning*, OECD Reviews of School Resources, OECD Publishing, Paris, https://dx.doi.org/10.1787/9789264276147-en. [14]

OECD (2013), *PISA 2012 Results: Excellence through Equity (Volume II): Giving Every Student the Chance to Succeed*, PISA, OECD Publishing, Paris, https://dx.doi.org/10.1787/9789264201132-en. [31]

OECD (2013), *Synergies for Better Learning: An International Perspective on Evaluation and Assessment*, OECD Reviews of Evaluation and Assessment in Education, OECD Publishing, Paris, https://dx.doi.org/10.1787/9789264190658-en. [9]

OECD (2011), *Quality Time for Students: Learning In and Out of School*, PISA, OECD Publishing, Paris, https://dx.doi.org/10.1787/9789264087057-en. [30]

OECD (2010), *PISA 2009 Results: What Students Know and Can Do: Student Performance in Reading, Mathematics and Science (Volume I)*, PISA, OECD Publishing, Paris, https://dx.doi.org/10.1787/9789264091450-en. [13]

OECD/The World Bank (2015), *OECD Reviews of School Resources: Kazakhstan 2015*, OECD Reviews of School Resources, OECD Publishing, Paris, https://dx.doi.org/10.1787/9789264245891-en. [18]

Pont, B., D. Nusche and H. Moorman (2008), *Improving School Leadership - Volume 1: Policy and Practice,*, OECD Publishing, Paris, https://www.oecd.org/education/school/improvingschoolleadership-volume1policyandpracticevolume2casestudiesonsystemleadership.htm (accessed on 20 January 2020). [17]

Rivkin, S. and J. Schiman (2015), "Instruction time, classroom quality, and academic achievement", *The Economic Journal*, Vol. 125/588, pp. F425-F448, http://dx.doi.org/10.1111/ecoj.12315. [23]

UNESCO-UIS (2018), *Education : Initial government funding of education per student as a percentage of GDP per capita*, http://data.uis.unesco.org/ (accessed on 4 July 2018). [12]

UNICEF (2017), *Improving Education Participation: Policy and Practice Pointers for Enrolling All Children and Adolescents in School and Preventing Dropout*, https://www.unicef.org/eca/media/2971/file/Improving_education_participation_report.pdf (accessed on 17 December 2020). [38]

UNICEF (2017), *UNICEF Calls for Ensuring Access to Quality Education for Every Child in Georgia*, https://www.unicef.org/georgia/press-releases/unicef-calls-ensuring-access-quality-education-every-child-georgia (accessed on 17 December 2020). [39]

UNICEF (2016), *Monitoring Education Participation: Framework for Monitoring Children and Adolescents who are Out of School or at Risk of Dropping Out*, https://www.unicef.org/eca/media/2956/file/monitoring_education_participation.pdf (accessed on 17 December 2020). [35]

UNICEF (2016), *UNICEF Annual Report: Bulgaria*, https://sites.unicef.org/about/annualreport/files/Bulgaria_2016_COAR.pdf (accessed on 25 February 2021). [42]

World Bank (2020), *Duration of compulsory education*, https://donnees.banquemondiale.org/indicateur/SE.COM.DURS (accessed on 7 December 2020). [32]

World Bank (2019), *Transforming the Education System in Croatia: Better Schools, Better Learning, Better Life*, http://documents1.worldbank.org/curated/en/360791554478893672/text/Concept-Project-Information-Document-PID-Transforming-the-Education-System-in-Croatia-Better-Schools-Better-Learning-Better-Life-P170178.txt (accessed on 9 April 2021). [27]

World Bank (2012), *Implementation Completion and Results Report - Education Sector Development Project*, http://documents1.worldbank.org/curated/en/544061468246325350/text/ICR22540Box3670disclosed04023020120.txt (accessed on 4 February 2021). [33]

Wu, D. (2020), "Disentangling the effects of the school year from the school day: Evidence from the TIMSS assessments", *Education Finance and Policy*, Vol. 15/1, pp. 104-135, http://dx.doi.org/10.1162/edfp_a_00265. [24]

Note

[1] A socio-economically disadvantaged (advantaged) school is a school in the bottom (top) quarter of the index of ESCS in the relevant country/economy.

3 Improving teaching

Introduction

In terms of education system-level factors, research suggests that teachers are one of the most important in impacting student outcomes (Hanushek, 2011[1]; Hattie, 2009[2]; Rivkin, Hanushek and Kain, 2005[3]). Many countries around the world have designed policies to prepare teachers and help them develop so they can become influential agents in improving student learning.

Several characteristics distinguish the teaching profession in the Eastern European and Central Asian (EECA) region. In many countries, teachers are comparatively older. Over one in four teachers in Georgia is over 60 (Li et al., 2019[4]), and Bulgaria and Georgia have two of the four oldest teaching populations out of all countries that participated in the most recent OECD Teaching and Learning International Survey (TALIS) (OECD, 2019[5]). Relative to international benchmarks, teachers in the EECA region also tend to have lower compensation compared to jobs that require similar educational qualifications (Kitchen et al., 2017[6]; OECD, 2017[7]) and be less satisfied with their salaries (OECD, 2019[5]). These factors shape the types of practices that teachers use, how they perceive their status in society and their motivation to improve, as well as the types of policies that EECA countries develop to support teachers.

This chapter uses the OECD Programme for International Student Assessment (PISA) data and other information to shed light on teachers, teaching and teacher policy in the EECA region. It begins by examining the types of practices that teachers use, and whether they are consistent with the methods that research shows foster inclusion and are effective in enabling student learning. It also examines how quality assurance mechanisms are functioning in the region and whether they might be reinforcing or complicating the implementation of desired teaching behaviours. Finally, this chapter looks at how countries in the region help their teachers improve, and what policy measures governments can consider to better support teachers in their national contexts.

Teaching practices

Broadly speaking, teachers in the EECA region continue to rely heavily on traditional pedagogy, such as lecturing to students and asking them to memorise information. Research suggests that these techniques might not be as well suited to developing some important skills and competences. In particular, international studies indicate that active, student-centred approaches might better help students develop so-called 21st century competences, such as creativity, critical thinking, collaborative problem solving and communication (Peterson et al., 2018[8]; Jacobs and Toh-Heng, 2013[9]). Moreover, traditional teaching practices can stand in the way of the personalised types of instruction that allow students to learn at their own pace and in different ways, which is especially important to making education more inclusive (OECD, 2012[10]). In response to these demands, many EECA countries are taking steps to modernise pedagogy and encourage teachers to adapt instruction to individual student needs.

International experience shows that changing teachers' classroom practice can be very challenging. One reason education systems often struggle to implement modern practices is because providers of initial teacher education (ITE) might not equip teacher candidates to use new approaches, often because programmes offer limited preparation in pedagogy and hands-on classroom practice (OECD, 2019[11]). Some EECA countries lack instruments, such as consistent programme accreditation and robust certification requirements. These instruments can help direct ITE providers to design programmes that align with national expectations for teaching and learning and guarantee minimum quality standards (OECD, 2020[12]).

Another reason is that more experienced teachers in the region might be hesitant to adopt newer approaches or need more support to adopt them. Many in-service teachers in the EECA region are older and were trained using very different pedagogical methods than what are expected today. These teachers need considerable support and incentives to adopt the desired, new approaches. Other sections in this chapter indicate the extent of these challenges, as well as some of the ways in which they might be overcome.

Data from PISA

Teaching methods in EECA countries (as perceived by students) are rather traditional and are associated with lower student achievement

The PISA 2018 student questionnaire asked students about how their teachers teach. Responses to these questions were used to construct five indices about teaching practices in students' language-of-instruction courses (Table 3.1). All indices are calculated to have an average of zero and standard deviation of one across OECD countries. Positive values in the indices mean that students perceived their reading teachers to be more enthusiastic, provide greater support or use certain teaching practices more frequently than what was reported by the average student across OECD countries (OECD, 2019[13]). Figure 3.1 shows the adjusted results[1] for these indices, which represent the extent to which each practice is more or less common relative to the others (and to the OECD average).

Table 3.1. Indices of teaching practice

Index name	Student prompt	Example questions
Teacher enthusiasm	Do you agree ("strongly agree", "agree", "disagree", "strongly disagree") with the following statements about the two language-of-instruction lessons you attended prior to sitting the PISA test?	It was clear to me that the teacher liked teaching us. The enthusiasm of the teacher inspired me.
Teacher support		The teacher shows an interest in every student's learning. The teacher gives extra help when students need it.
Teacher feedback		The teacher gives me feedback on my strengths in this subject. The teacher tells me in which areas I can improve.
Teacher-directed instruction	How often ("never or hardly never", "some lessons", "most lessons", "every lesson") do the following happen in your language-of-instruction lessons?	The teacher asks questions to check whether we have understood what was taught. The teacher tells us what we have to learn.
Adaptive instruction		The teacher adapts the lesson to [my] class's needs and knowledge. The teacher changes the structure of the lesson on a topic that most students find difficult to understand.

Source: (OECD, 2019[14]), *PISA 2018 Database*, https://www.oecd.org/pisa/data/2018database/ (accessed 17 November 2020).

Figure 3.1. Teacher practices

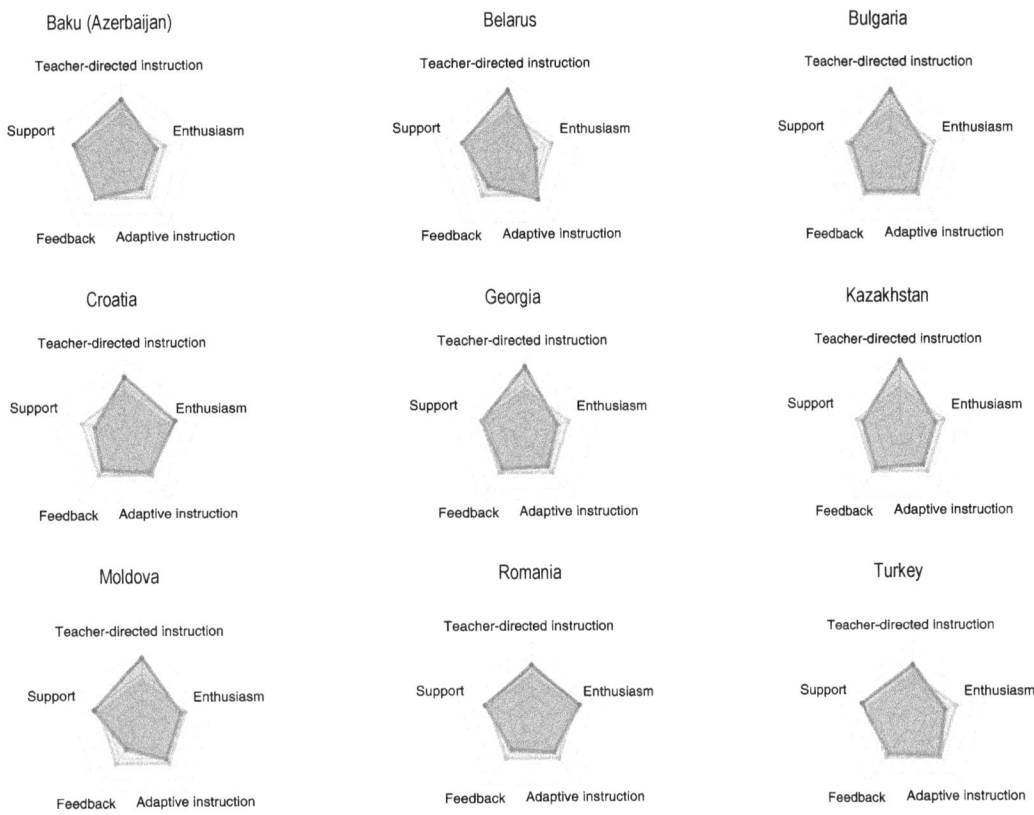

Note: Data were missing for Ukraine.
Source: (OECD, 2019[14]), PISA 2018 database, https://www.oecd.org/pisa/data/2018database/ (accessed 17 November 2020).

In all nine EECA countries with data, teacher-directed instruction is more common compared to the OECD average, and there is generally less adaptive instruction and teacher enthusiasm (Box 3.1). In all EECA countries with data, students who reported experiencing more adaptive practices in language-of-instruction lessons experienced greater increases in reading, even after accounting for gender and socio-economic status (Figure 3.2). In all countries except Kazakhstan, students had lower outcomes in reading with greater exposure to teacher-directed instruction.

Figure 3.2. Teacher practices and reading performance

Change in reading performance associated with greater student exposure to:

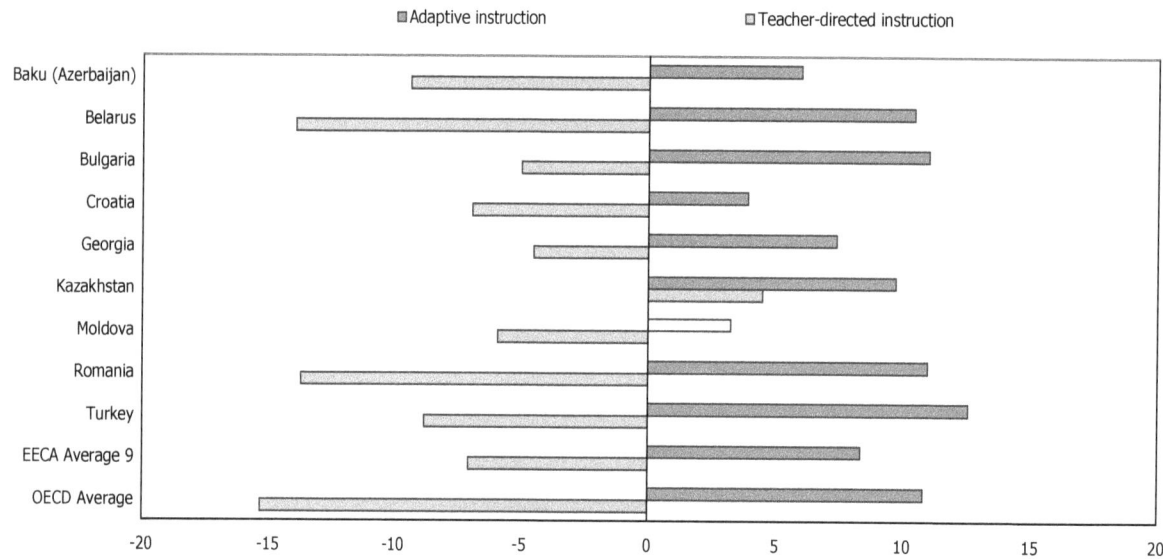

Notes: Results based on linear regression analysis after accounting for gender and students' and schools' socio-economic status.
Values that are statistically significant are shaded.
The data for this figure were collected before Costa Rica became an OECD member.
Source: (OECD, 2019[14]), *PISA 2018 database*, https://www.oecd.org/pisa/data/2018database/ (accessed 17 November 2020).

StatLink https://stat.link/xof674

Box 3.1. Teacher enthusiasm

In EECA countries, teacher enthusiasm is perceived as lower overall compared to the OECD average, except in Croatia and Romania. Students who scored higher in reading were more likely to perceive their teacher as enthusiastic in all EECA countries except in Kazakhstan, after accounting for the socio-economic status of students and schools.

However, researchers note that the relationship between teacher enthusiasm and student performance is probably indirect and moderated by other factors (OECD, 2020[15]). For example, in all PISA-participating countries and economies, disciplinary climate and student motivation were positively associated with teacher enthusiasm, and the directionality of these relationships is unclear. Students may be more motivated and behave better with a more enthusiastic teacher, or a teacher might be more enthusiastic with more motivated and better-disciplined students (OECD, 2019[13]). After accounting for disciplinary climate and students' motivation to master tasks, the association between student performance and teacher enthusiasm disappears in all EECA countries except Baku (Azerbaijan) and Belarus (ibid).

Some teacher behaviours that are more common in the EECA region may hinder student learning

PISA 2018 asked school principals to report on the extent to which they think that student learning in their schools is hindered by:

- School staff resisting change
- Teacher absenteeism
- Teachers not meeting individual students' needs
- Teachers not being well-prepared for classes

Principals in most EECA countries are more likely to report that these teacher behaviours, especially teacher absenteeism and lack of preparation, hinder student learning (Figure 3.3). Kazakhstan reported the highest rates of such concern across all PISA-participating countries – 40% of students attend schools where principals think that learning is hindered a lot by teacher absenteeism (the OECD average is 3%) and 44% attend schools where the principals report that teachers not being well-prepared for classes hinders learning a lot (the OECD average is 2%). These results can be partially explained by the difficulty in allocating teacher capacity efficiently in the vast Kazakhstani school network (even if the total number of teachers is adequate), and the lack of quality assurance in a highly fragmented ITE system (OECD, 2020[12]).

Figure 3.3. Teacher behaviour that may hinder student learning

Percentage of students whose principal reported that the following behaviours hindered student learning a lot in their schools

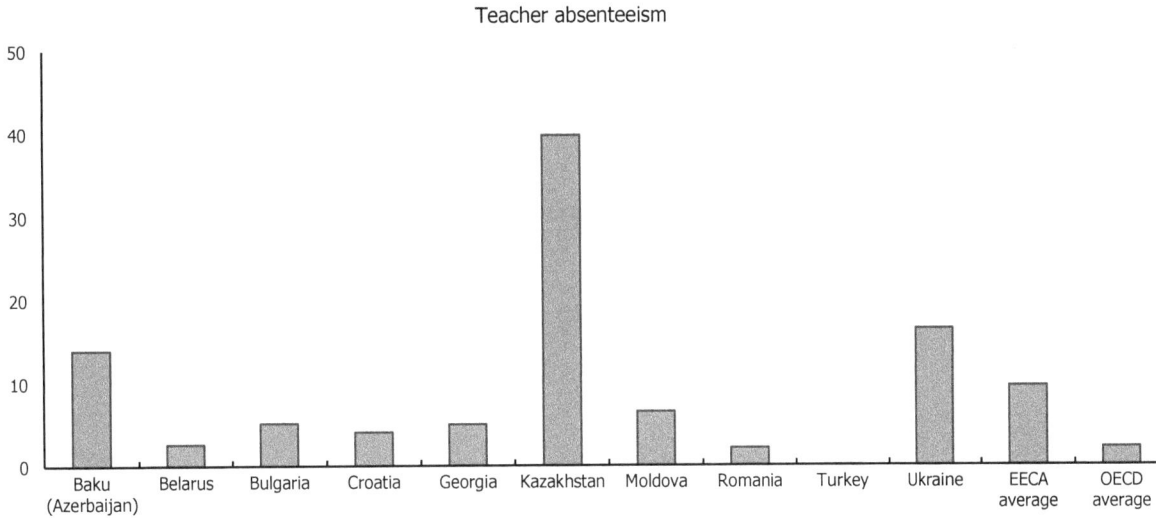

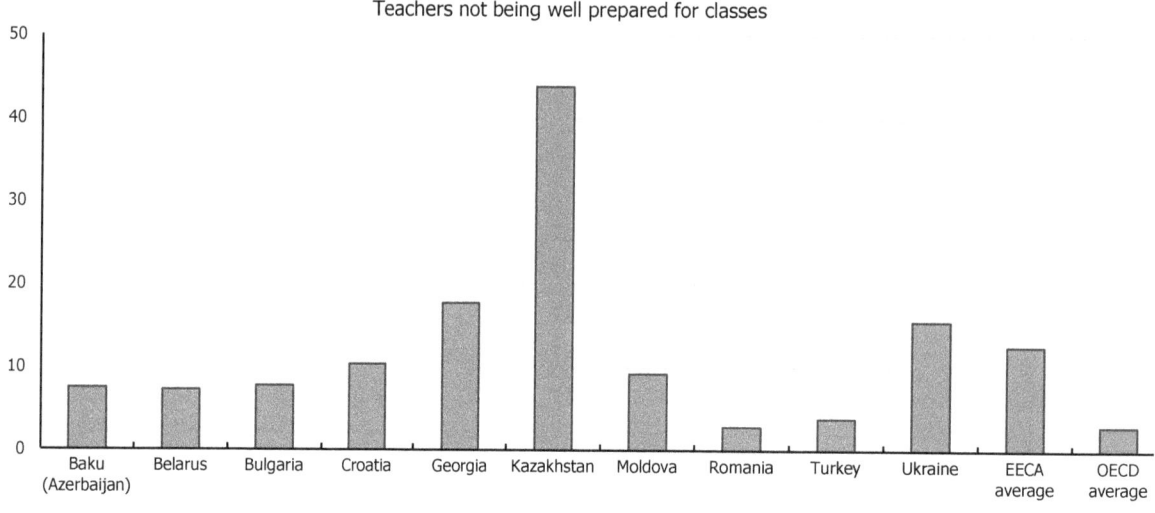

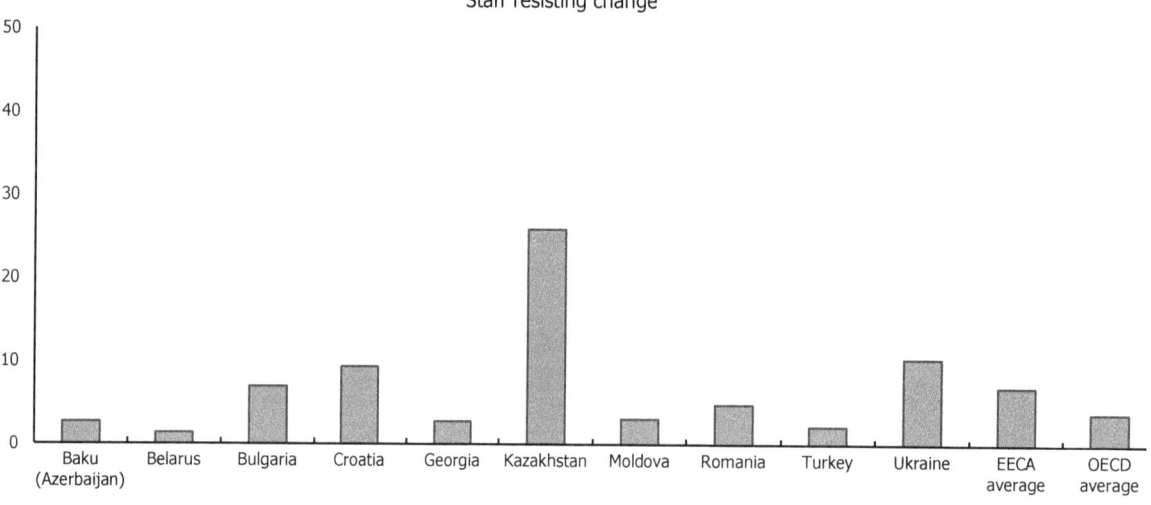

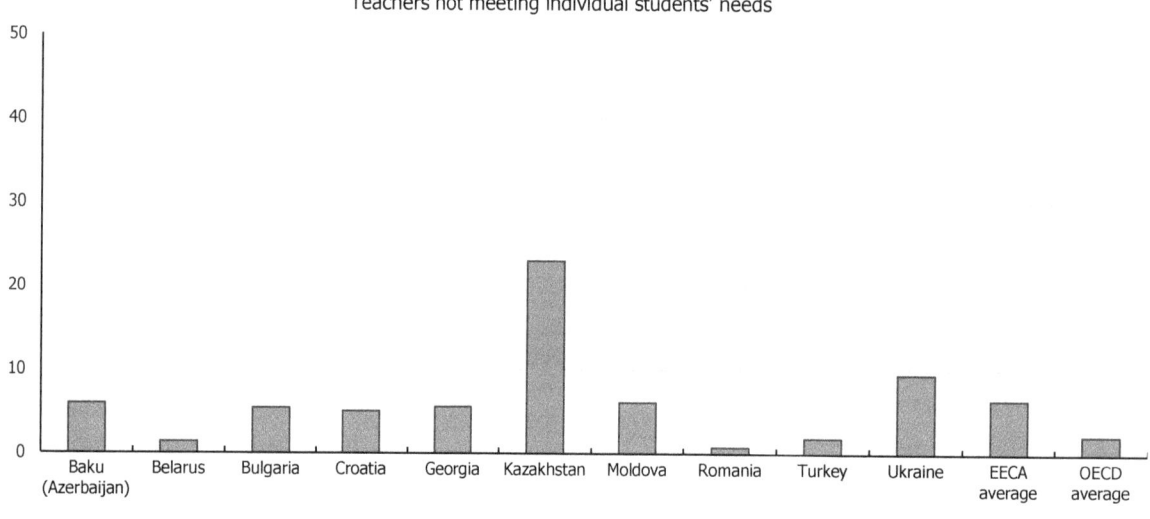

Note: The data for this figure were collected before Costa Rica became an OECD member.
Source: (OECD, 2019[14]), *PISA 2018 Database*, Table III.B1.7.1, https://www.oecd.org/pisa/data/2018database/ (accessed 17 November 2020)

StatLink https://stat.link/7twnci

Policy implications

Teacher standards can help set out desired teaching practices

Standards are an effective (and among OECD countries, common) way of aligning teacher policies and practices as they represent a common reference point that anchors the overall understanding of teacher responsibilities and expected performance (OECD, 2013[16]). Teacher standards describe what teachers should know and be able to do, including the description of a desirable level of performance (Ingvarson, 2002[17]). These standards can help inform initial teacher education, certification, appraisal and professional development by aligning institutions and practices around a shared vision of teaching.

Some EECA countries have created national standards to help guide the profession (Table 3.2). In general, these standards positively feature key pedagogical knowledge and skills and highlight important practices, such as individualised and adaptive instruction. Many also set out different levels of the teaching profession (e.g. beginner and advanced), which is important in this region because in many countries teachers also assume school leadership roles (see Chapter 2).

Nevertheless, there are issues regarding the extensiveness and relevance of teacher standards across the region. Azerbaijan and Croatia do not yet have comprehensive, modern teacher standards. Belarus relies upon occupational characteristics, which act more like job descriptions rather than providing explicit expectations of the knowledge and competences teachers should demonstrate (Ministry of Education of the Republic of Belarus, 2011[18]). Similarly, Romania introduced a Teaching Staff Statute that sets out the formal qualifications to be a teacher, as well as their rights and obligations, but not the competences that teachers are expected to master in order to be effective, classroom instructors (Kitchen et al., 2017[6]). Developing modern, multidimensional teacher standards in these countries can help promote a common understanding of what good teaching is, and what practices teachers are expected to use in the classroom. Other sections in this chapter discuss further what policies countries can consider to help implement and embed teacher standards.

Table 3.2. Teacher standards in EECA countries

	Year when teacher standards were introduced
Baku (Azerbaijan)	N/A
Belarus	N/A (Occupational characteristics in 2013, standards expected to be developed in 2021)
Bulgaria	2019
Croatia	N/A
Georgia	2015
Kazakhstan	2017
Moldova	2018
Romania	N/A (Teaching Staff Statute in 2012)
Turkey	2017
Ukraine	2020

Sources: (European CommissionEACEA/Eurydice, 2020[19]), *Compulsory Education in Europe – 2020/21. Eurydice Facts and Figures*, http://dx.doi.org/10.2797/20126; (Kitchen et al., 2017[6]), *OECD Reviews of Evaluation and Assessment: Romania*, https://dx.doi.org/10.1787/9789264274051-en, (Kitchen et al., 2019[20]), *OECD Reviews of Evaluation and Assessment: Student Assessment in Turkey*, https://dx.doi.org/10.1787/5edc0abe-en; Law on Education in Primary and Secondary School in Croatia (2020). https://www.zakon.hr/z/317/Zakon-o-odgoju-i-obrazovanju-u-osnovnoj-i-srednjoj-%C5%A1koli (accessed 23 April 2021); (Li et al., 2019[4]), *OECD Reviews of Evaluation and Assessment: Georgia*, https://dx.doi.org/10.1787/94dc370e-en, (OECD, 2020[21]), *Raising the quality of initial teacher education and support for early career teachers in Kazakhstan*, https://doi.org/10.1787/68c45a81-en.

Professional codes of conduct can complement teacher standards

A growing number of countries have developed a professional code of conduct for teachers to accompany their teacher standards. While teacher standards set out expectations for teachers' professional competences, codes of conduct help communicate what these expectations mean in day-to-day practice, and also set out expectations for teachers' integrity and disposition. For example, in Scotland (United Kingdom), the teacher code of conduct asks teachers to act role models to students and not engage in dishonest activities (GTC Scotland, 2012[22]). Guidelines like these can help develop awareness among teachers about what the core values of the profession are and how they are expected to conduct themselves in unexpected situations.

Establishing codes of conduct might be especially relevant in EECA countries because there are concerns about the integrity of teacher activities, particularly regarding absenteeism or offering private tutoring to students, and how those activities can affect their classroom behaviour (OECD, 2017[7]). Moreover, in some EECA countries responsibility for hiring and dismissing teachers rests almost solely with the school itself. In Bulgaria, Croatia and Georgia, over 94% of principals in lower secondary schools are responsible for appointing or hiring teachers, compared to 70% across the OECD (OECD, 2019[5]). This autonomy around staffing can create issues around fairness and transparency, especially in the types of small, rural communities that are common in many parts of the EECA region (and also increase the need to develop the capacity of school leaders, see Chapter 2) (Li et al., 2019[4]). Having a code of conduct could help schools and teachers in these situations make difficult decisions in a more impartial manner, and be held more accountable for the decisions they make.

Teacher qualifications

Countries can help make sure that teachers have the competences needed to teach in the classroom through several methods. A common approach is to introduce requirements that teachers must meet in order to be certified, such as holding a minimum educational qualification. While requiring teachers to have a certain level of education (or in some cases encouraging them to have higher-than-minimum levels) does not necessarily imply higher quality teaching, most OECD countries require teachers to hold at least a Bachelor's degree, though Master's degrees are increasingly mandatory to teach certain subjects or grade levels. Other certification requirements include asking ITE graduates[2] to pass a certification examination that is aligned with teacher standards, and/or implementing compulsory probationary periods.

Examples of these types of requirements are present in some EECA countries (Table 3.3), though many parts of the region have yet to introduce such quality assurance measures. In countries where qualification and certification standards exist, they have been introduced fairly recently, leaving many in-service teachers with very different qualification levels.

Table 3.3. Requirements to become a fully certified teacher

	Level of education	Passing a central examination after ITE	Completion of a probationary period
Baku (Azerbaijan)	Bachelor (or sub-Bachelor if trained in a college)	X	
Belarus	Specialist or Master		
Bulgaria	Bachelor	X	
Croatia	Bachelor (Master for upper levels)		X
Georgia	Bachelor	X	
Kazakhstan	Bachelor	X (in 2021)	
Moldova	Bachelor (Master for upper secondary)		
Romania	Bachelor	X	X

Turkey	Bachelor	X	X
Ukraine	Bachelor or a professional qualification		X (internship)

Sources: (European CommissionEACEA/Eurydice, 2020[19])), *Compulsory Education in Europe – 2020/21. Eurydice Facts and Figures*, http://dx.doi.org/10.2797/20126, (Kitchen et al., 2017[6]), *OECD Reviews of Evaluation and Assessment: Romania*, https://dx.doi.org/10.1787/9789264274051-en; (Kitchen et al., 2019[20]), *OECD Reviews of Evaluation and Assessment: Student Assessment in Turkey*, https://dx.doi.org/10.1787/5edc0abe-en, (Li et al., 2019[4]), *OECD Reviews of Evaluation and Assessment: Georgia*, https://dx.doi.org/10.1787/94dc370e-en, (OECD, 2020[21]), *Raising the quality of initial teacher education and support for early career teachers in Kazakhstan*, https://doi.org/10.1787/68c45a81-en, Ukraine Ministry of Economic Development, Trade and Agriculture (2020), *Professional Standard of a Primary School Teacher, and a Teacher of a General Secondary Education Institution*, https://www.me.gov.ua/Documents/Detail?lang=uk-UA&id=22469103-4e36-4d41-b1bf-288338b3c7fa&title=RestrProfesiinikhStandartiv, (accessed 23 April 2021).

Data from PISA

Teachers in EECA countries are as likely to be certified and hold a Master's degree as teachers in OECD countries

PISA 2018 asked school principals to report the number of teachers in their schools who are "fully certified by an appropriate authority", and the number of teachers who hold advanced qualifications[3]. Almost all EECA countries with data have a share of fully certified teachers above the OECD average (see Figure 3.4). The exception is Georgia, which has one of the lowest shares of certified teachers among all PISA-participating countries. Georgia's low rate might be related to the difficulty the country has had in implementing a new teacher certification scheme, particularly among older in-service teachers, that was introduced in 2015 (Li et al., 2019[4]). It should be noted that education systems create their own definition for "full certification" in PISA, meaning that requirements can vary across systems. For instance, certification could signal that a teacher has received an ITE qualification, accumulated a minimum number of student-teaching hours, passed an exam, some combination of these criteria, or none of them.

On average in the EECA region 49% of teachers hold a Master's degree, which is similar to the OECD average, but there are large differences between countries. While over 70% of teachers in Bulgaria, Croatia and Ukraine have a Master's degree, only 2% do in Belarus, 16% in Turkey and 20% in Moldova. The low values in Belarus and Moldova might be related to the fact that many teachers hold five-year "specialist" degrees, which are not always classified as Master's degrees for international benchmarking purposes.

Figure 3.4. Teacher qualifications

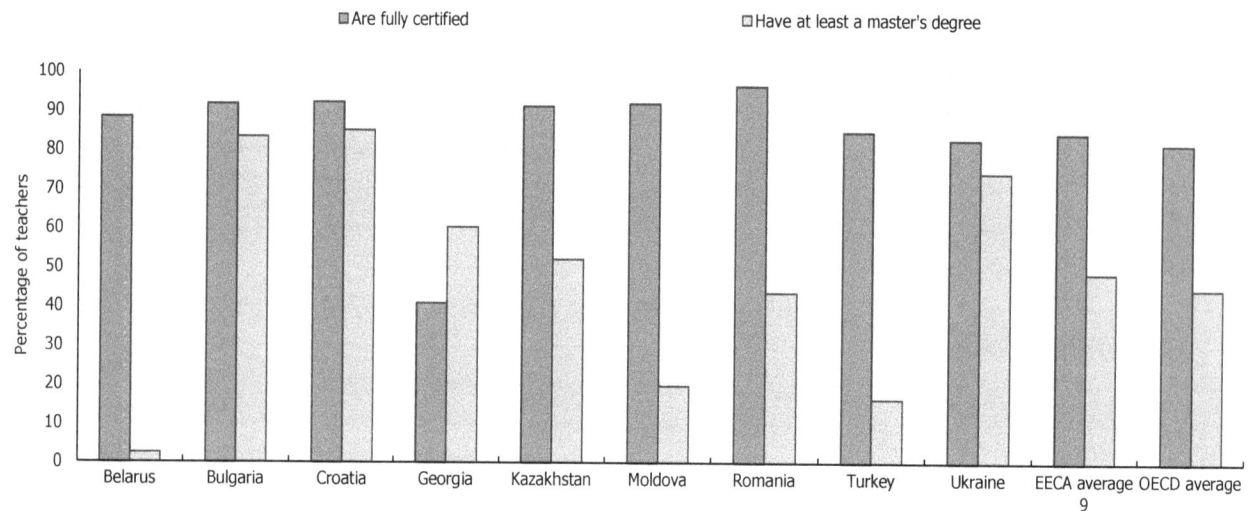

Notes: Based on principals' reports.
Baku (Azerbaijan) is not included since the majority of data were missing.
The data for this figure were collected before Costa Rica became an OECD member.
Source: (OECD, 2019[14]), *PISA 2018 database*, https://www.oecd.org/pisa/data/2018database/ (accessed 17 November 2020).

StatLink https://stat.link/n72rjd

The most qualified teachers in EECA countries are disproportionately concentrated in urban schools

Highly qualified teachers are a valuable resource and it is important that they be allocated where they can achieve the greatest and most equitable outcomes. Internationally, the share of fully certified teachers is similar across socio-economically advantaged and disadvantaged schools and rural and urban schools (Figure 3.5). This trend is also found across EECA countries, which is likely reflective of the relatively high overall rates of certification across the region. There are, however, a few noteworthy exceptions. In Georgia and Ukraine, socio-economically advantaged schools have a greater share of fully certified teachers, while in Turkey socio-economically disadvantaged schools do.

A greater disparity can be seen with respect to teachers who hold at least a Master's degree. Across OECD countries, socio-economically advantaged schools have more teachers with at least a Master's degree by 10 percentage points. The difference in EECA countries is 9 percentage points, but the gap is particularly wide in Moldova (24 percentage points), Bulgaria (16 percentage points) and Romania (also 16 percentage points). In EECA countries with a large share of rural students, schools in urban areas have greater shares of teachers with at least a Master's degree (by 16 percentage points, compared to 10 across similar OECD countries). The gap is particularly large in Kazakhstan (34 percentage points) and Romania (20 percentage points).

Several reasons can help explain why better-educated teachers tend to be found in socio-economically advantaged and urban schools. Universities that can support advanced degree programs are more likely to be located in urban areas and newly graduated teachers might wish to work close to where they have established their homes. Socio-economically advantaged and urban schools might offer better teaching conditions and can better attract the most competitive candidates (OECD, 2019[23]). These factors help explain why teachers in some EECA countries who work in disadvantaged schools are more likely to want to change schools more than teachers who work in advantaged schools (OECD, 2019[5]). Without effective policy interventions to deliberately allocate teachers to certain areas, these trends can contribute to inequities in student achievement, especially in EECA countries, which have larger shares of rural schools and struggle with equitable school resourcing (see Chapter 2).

Figure 3.5. Percentage of fully certified teachers, by school characteristics

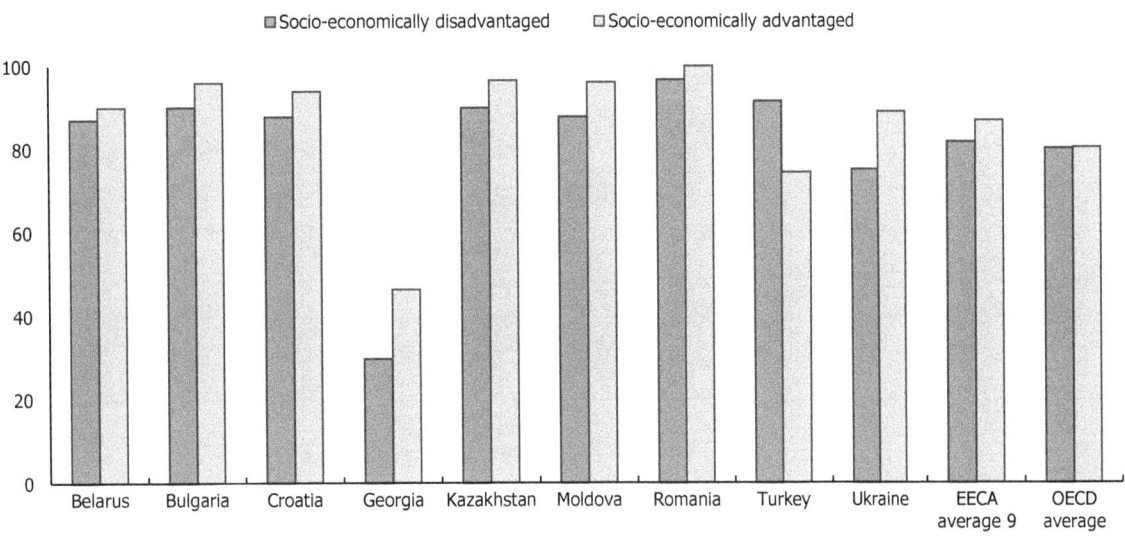

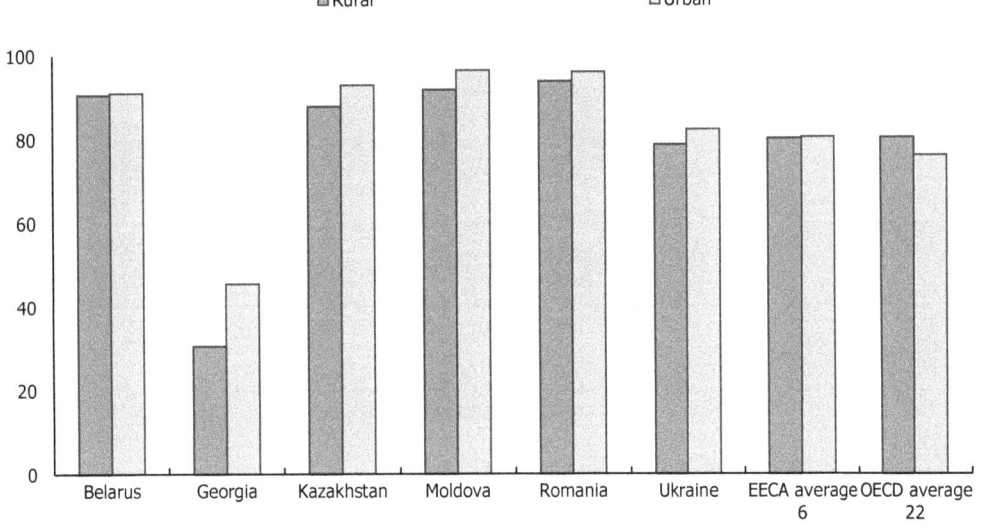

Notes: Missing countries on the bottom part of the figure had 3% or less of 15-year-old students enrolled in rural schools (hence "EECA average 6" and "OECD average 22").
The data for this figure were collected before Costa Rica became an OECD member.
Source: (OECD, 2019[14]), *PISA 2018 database*, https://www.oecd.org/pisa/data/2018database/ (accessed 17 November 2020).

StatLink https://stat.link/pc73qg

Figure 3.6. Percentage of teachers with at least a Master's degree, by school characteristics

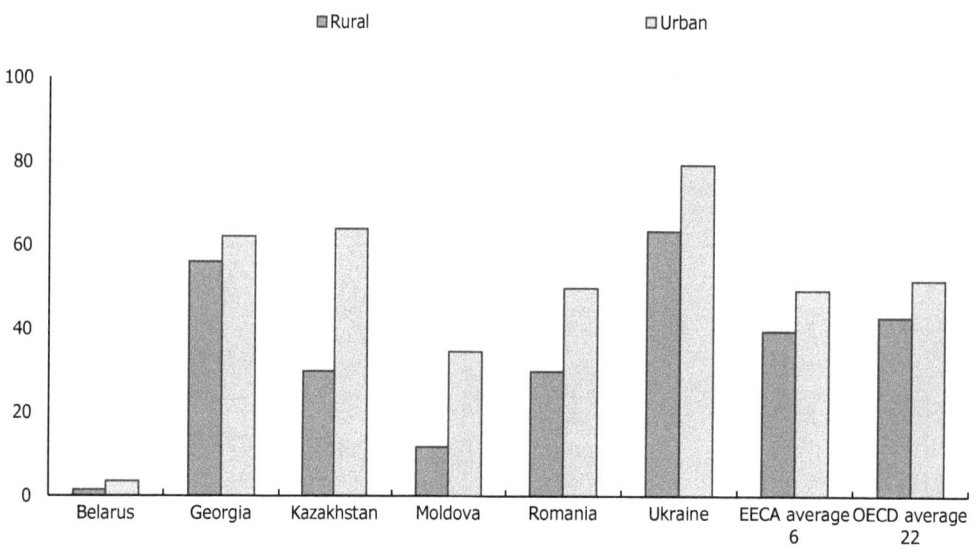

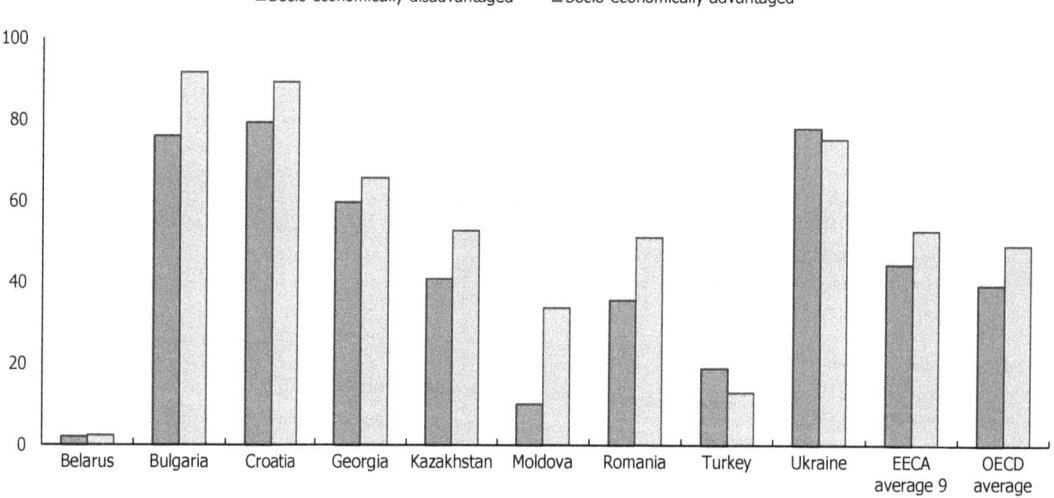

Notes: Missing countries on the top part of the figure had 3% or less of 15-year-old students enrolled in rural schools (hence "EECA average 6" and "OECD average 22").
The data for these figures were collected before Costa Rica became an OECD member.
Source: (OECD, 2019[14]), PISA 2018 database, https://www.oecd.org/pisa/data/2018database/ (accessed 17 November 2020).

StatLink ⟶ https://stat.link/a8bu2p

There is little relationship between teacher qualifications and student outcomes or the use of modern teaching practices in EECA countries

Implicit in policies about teacher qualifications is the belief that better qualified teachers help improve student outcomes. Countries trust that acquiring qualifications is an indicator that teachers can help students learn. Internationally, PISA data show that there is a positive relationship between teacher qualifications and student learning. Students from schools with greater shares of teachers who are fully certified and who have Master's degrees tend to have higher performance, even after accounting for the students' and schools' socio-economic status.

In EECA countries, the results are less conclusive. On average across the region, there is no relationship between the share of certified teachers in a school and student performance, after accounting for student and school socio-economic status, though there is a positive relationship in Bulgaria, Georgia and Turkey. This more varied picture might in part be explained by issues with the quality of teacher education in the region and the lack of robust quality assurance (Kitchen et al., 2017[6]; OECD, 2020[12]). Across the region, there is a positive relationship between the share of teachers with a Master's degree and student outcomes, after accounting for student and school socio-economic status, though this relationship is driven strongly by Turkey (in Kazakhstan and Moldova the relationship is also positive).

Figure 3.7. Teacher qualifications and reading outcomes

Change in reading performance for every 10% increase in the share of teachers who:

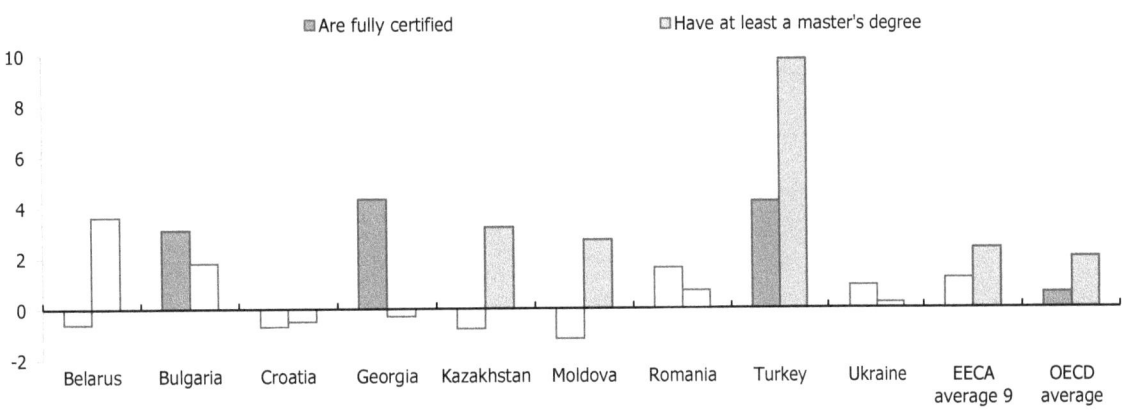

Notes: Baku (Azerbaijan) is not included since the majority of data were missing.
Values that are statistically significant are shaded.
The data for these figures were collected before Costa Rica became an OECD member.
Source: (OECD, 2019[14]), *PISA 2018 database*, https://www.oecd.org/pisa/data/2018database/ (accessed 17 November 2020).

StatLink https://stat.link/mewgyf

With respect to teaching practice, there is no relationship on average between teacher qualifications and the use of adaptive instruction (Figure 3.8). The exceptions are Bulgaria, where the share of certified teachers is positively correlated with more adaptive instruction, Turkey, where the share of teacher's with a Master's degree is associated with more adaptive instruction, and Kazakhstan, where the share of teacher's with a Master's degree is associated with both more teacher-directed and adaptive instruction. These findings provide further evidence that certification and educational requirements in the EECA region are not always adequate and highlight the need to make the mechanisms more accurately signal high-quality teaching.

Figure 3.8. Teacher qualifications and teacher practices

Change in teacher practices for every 10% increase in the share of teachers who:

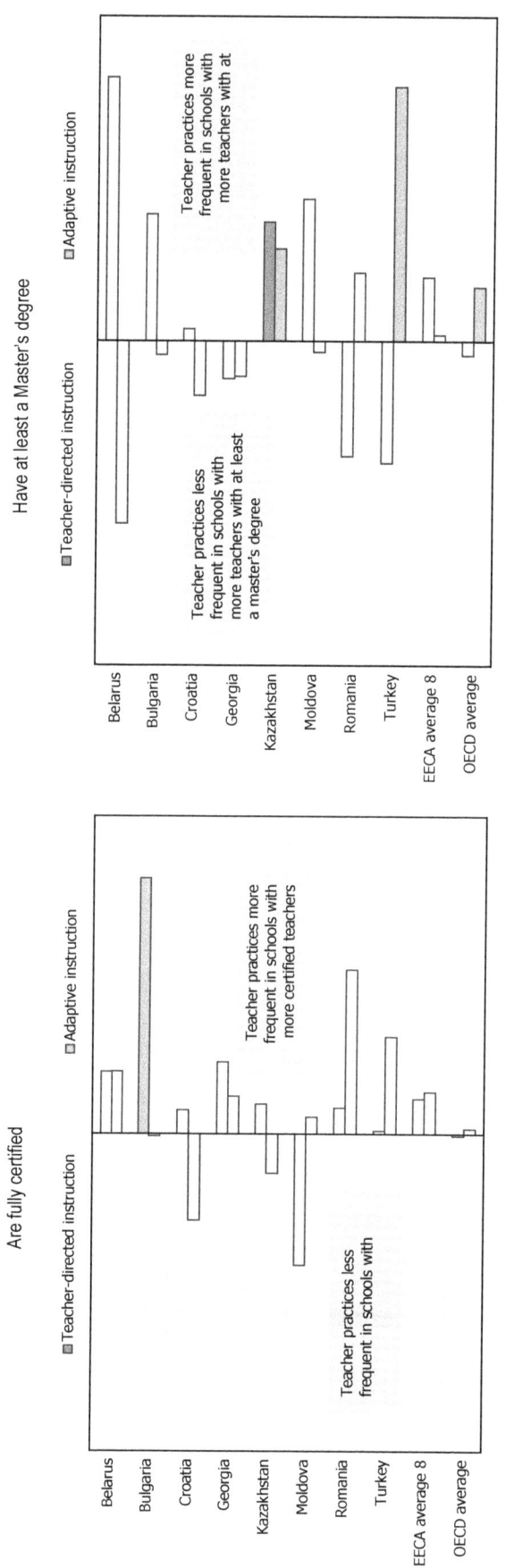

Notes: Baku (Azerbaijan) is not included since the majority of data were missing. No data for Ukraine were available.
Values that are statistically significant are shaded.
The data for these figures were collected before Costa Rica became an OECD member.
Source: (OECD, 2019[14]), *PISA 2018 database*, https://www.oecd.org/pisa/data/2018database/ (accessed 17 November 2020).

StatLink https://stat.link/203sjp

Policy implications

Attracting high-quality teaching candidates and improving initial teacher education programmes can help strengthen the link between teacher qualifications and classroom practices

EECA countries should address issues that might be affecting the value and quality of ITE, so holding certain teacher qualifications can more reliably signal good teaching. While there are several approaches that countries can consider, two important reforms are strengthening the intake of students into ITE programmes, and improving the quality of the programmes themselves.

Student intake

United Nations Children's Fund (UNICEF)-OECD policy reviews have revealed that, in many countries in the region, entry into regional ITE programmes is not very selective, which is partly a reflection of the perceived status of the teaching profession in the region. In Georgia, for example, entrants into four-year, concurrent ITE programmes often had lower scores on the former national entrance examination than students who enrolled in other programmes (Li et al., 2019[4]). A similar situation is observed in Ukraine (OECD, 2017[7]). These circumstances are problematic because individuals entering ITE might have lower academic abilities, and some may not regard teaching as their first career choice, and thus not be highly motivated to teach. Tertiary faculty might spend valuable learning time teaching candidates basic content knowledge and how to be good students, rather than how to be good teachers.

Some countries in the region are taking steps to improve the quality of students who enter ITE programmes. For example, in 2020 Kazakhstan raised the minimum required score on the national entrance examination by 10 points (out of a possible 100) for ITE programmes, which makes it 20 points higher than the minimum score needed to enter tertiary education in general. It should be noted, however, that Kazakhstan has a relatively young teacher population compared to some countries in the region. Therefore, there is less risk of encountering teacher shortages by raising ITE entrance standards, and more value to be gained by doing so. Georgia, which has much older teacher workforce, is emphasising a recently introduced consecutive programme that focuses on developing the pedagogical skills of candidates and mid-career professionals who have already acquired subject matter expertise (Li et al., 2019[4]).

ITE quality assurance

Findings from the UNICEF-OECD policy reviews suggest that ITE programmes in EECA countries are often characterised by fragmentation. Weak quality assurance, combined in some countries with a sparsely distributed population across a large territory, has led to a large variety of ITE providers, each with differing levels of quality. In Kazakhstan, for example, ITE is offered at 86 universities and 277 teacher colleges (OECD, 2020[21]). A majority of Romania's 83 universities offer some form of ITE (Kitchen et al., 2017[6]).

To address issues related to ensuring the quality of diverse ITE offerings, several EECA countries have introduced quality assurance mechanisms at several stages of the ITE process. Two important mechanisms are programme accreditation and certification examinations.

- Programme accreditation – Strong accreditation processes that are aligned with teacher standards give ITE providers a common reference point around which to build their curricula. In Kazakhstan, ten separate organisations accredit ITE programmes, but the country is moving towards focusing on two in order to ensure more consistent, high-quality ITE (OECD, 2020[21]). In Turkey, the Evaluation and Accreditation Association of Educational Faculty Programs will act as the external accrediting body for ITE and sets accreditation requirements (Kitchen et al., 2019[24]).

- Certification examinations – When properly designed and aligned with national teacher standards, certification examinations can act as an important, external validation that teacher candidates, regardless of where they were trained, have the knowledge and competences needed to be effective teachers. They can be particularly important when institutional quality assurance is weak and/or there are concerns around the integrity of teacher appointment processes. Only four EECA countries currently administer such examinations, though Kazakhstan is planning to introduce one in 2021 (Table 3.3).

Introducing mandatory probation can help validate teachers' knowledge and skills in an authentic environment

In many OECD countries, teachers are not fully certified until they complete a mandatory probation period. This process can help teachers develop their skills in real-life situations, and allow schools to make a more informed decision about whether a teacher is ready to work in a particular environment (OECD, 2013[16]). Given the fragmentation of the ITE landscape in some EECA countries, introducing probation periods can be a particularly valuable policy consideration.

Only three out of ten EECA countries require teachers to pass a probationary period before becoming fully certified (a fourth requires an internship) (Table 3.3). However, teacher mentorship is well established in the professional culture of the region. In Kazakhstan, for example, 97% of lower secondary principals report that their schools have some kind of mentoring programme, as do 93% of principals in Croatia (the average of 30 OECD countries is 64%) (OECD, 2019[5]). Policymakers in these countries can leverage these existing mechanisms and combine them with national teacher standards and career structures to create more formal probationary processes for new teachers.

Incentivising teachers to work in high need areas can make teacher allocation more equitable

Some OECD countries have introduced financial incentives to encourage teachers to work in areas where they are most needed, such as setting higher salaries for teaching in schools that have greater shares of students from disadvantaged backgrounds (OECD, 2019[23]). While these efforts are not always successful at equitably allocating teachers (in-school support can improve the impact of these policies) (ibid), they can be considered in the EECA region, where teacher salaries are comparatively lower and many countries are already exploring ways to boost compensation (see section on Professional development).

Belarus's recently revised teacher compensation scheme increases a teacher's salary if they work in rural areas, with students from more vulnerable backgrounds, such as those from economically disadvantaged families and those who are orphans (Ministry of Education of the Republic of Belarus, 2019[25]). However, it should be noted that these salary supplements are still generally lower than those given for teaching students who compete in Olympiads, which could moderate the policy's effectiveness. Kazakhstan has invested resources on more equitably allocating teachers immediately after ITE. The country has created a scholarship program that funds teacher candidates' ITE on the condition that they teach for at least three years in rural areas (OECD/The World Bank, 2015[26]).

Professional development

Education systems need to help teachers keep their skills up-to-date in relation to system-wide goals and expectations. It is therefore crucial that teachers have access to meaningful and relevant professional development opportunities, both school-based and externally provided, that align with teacher standards and broader education priorities. However, data from PISA and UNICEF-OECD policy reviews reveal that professional development in EECA countries is lower than international comparisons, especially for teachers who teach in more disadvantaged contexts. Without greater commitment to equitable and effective professional development, countries in the region will likely have continued difficulty in improving teaching and learning.

Data from PISA

Teachers in EECA countries, especially those who work in disadvantaged requirements, are less likely to participate in professional development

Results from PISA 2018 suggest that, on average, teachers in EECA countries participate in professional development at lower rates compared to international benchmarks (Figure 3.9). Only teachers in Bulgaria and Croatia participated in professional development at rates comparable to the OECD average, while teachers in Belarus participated in professional development the least of all PISA-participating countries. Turkey's comparatively lower rate might be partially explained by the fact that professional development is generally not mandatory for teachers (Kitchen et al., 2019[20]).

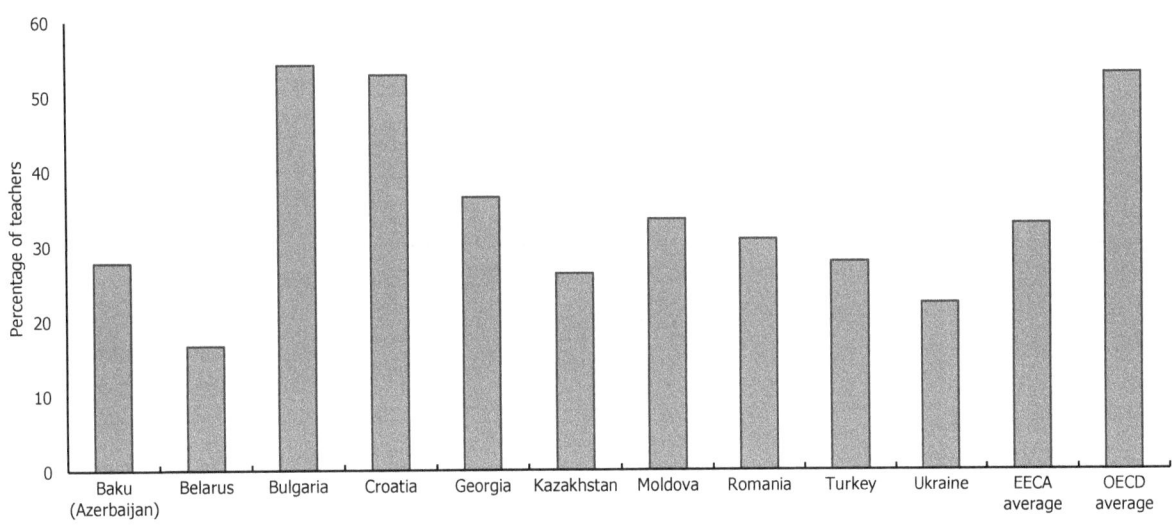

Figure 3.9. Percentage of teachers who participate in professional development

Notes: Based on principals' reports.
The data for these figures were collected before Costa Rica became an OECD member.
Source: (OECD, 2019[14]), *PISA 2018 database*, https://www.oecd.org/pisa/data/2018database/ (accessed 17 November 2020).

StatLink ▰▱▰ https://stat.link/qzd7h8

An important question regarding professional development is to whom it is made available. Availability is particularly important for teachers who work in disadvantaged environments, as they might need more support to effectively teach their students. Looking at the difference between advantaged and disadvantaged schools, in Croatia and Turkey more teachers from socio-economically advantaged schools attended professional development in the last three months compared to teachers in socio-economically disadvantaged schools (Figure 3.10). Evidence from PISA shows that teachers in urban schools in Kazakhstan are more likely to attend professional development than those in schools located in rural areas. In other countries with large shares of rural students there was no difference. Evidence from TALIS 2018 shows that in Georgia and Romania teachers who teach in urban schools are more likely to participate in professional development activities than their colleagues teaching in rural schools (OECD, 2019[5]).

Figure 3.10. Participation in professional development by school type

Difference between socio-economically advantaged and disadvantaged schools according to:

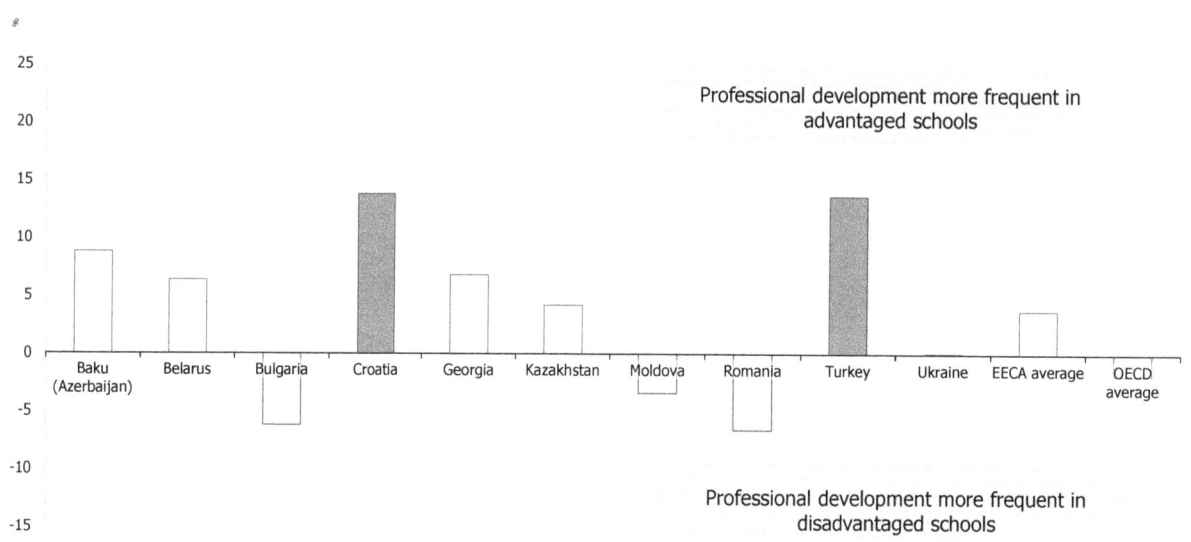

Notes: Values that are statistically significant are shaded.
The data for these figures were collected before Costa Rica became an OECD member.
Source: (OECD, 2019[14]), *PISA 2018 Database*, https://www.oecd.org/pisa/data/2018database/ (accessed 17 November 2020).

StatLink ⟶ https://stat.link/rspmb9

Links between professional development and desired teaching practices are weak

Across the OECD, data from PISA reveal a positive association between the amount of professional development teachers receive and how frequently they use adaptive instruction (Figure 3.11). In EECA countries, however, the trend is less conclusive. In no country was there an association between more professional development and greater use of adaptive instruction. However, students in schools where teachers participate in more professional development, especially those in Georgia and Turkey, tended to report less teacher-directed instruction. These findings are corroborated by TALIS 2018 results. A smaller share of lower secondary teachers from Bulgaria and Turkey (compared to the OECD average) feel that professional development activities had a positive impact on their teaching practices (OECD, 2019[5]).

Figure 3.11. Professional development and teacher practices

Change in teacher practices for every 10% increase in the share of teachers who participate in professional development

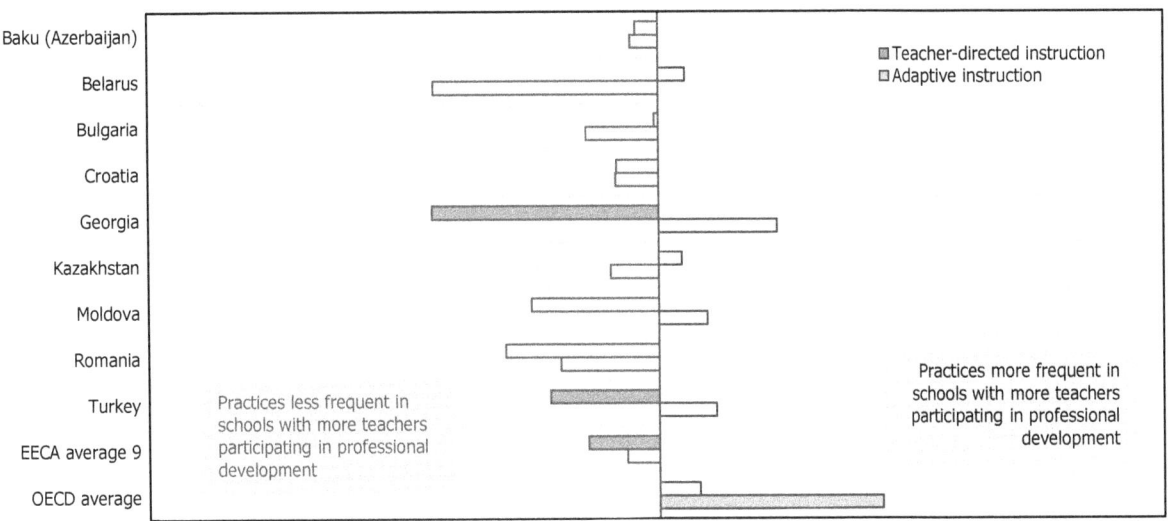

Notes: Values that are statistically significant are shaded.
The data for these figures were collected before Costa Rica became an OECD member.
Source: (OECD, 2019[14]), *PISA 2018 Database*, https://www.oecd.org/pisa/data/2018database/ (accessed 17 November 2020).

StatLink https://stat.link/gwh47d

Findings from UNICEF-OECD policy reviews offer several possible explanations for why professional development in the EECA region might not be consistently supporting teachers to use modern teaching practices. One issue is that, as previously mentioned, teacher standards are not widely implemented in the EECA region (see Table 3.2). Without a system-wide reference point, training providers might not know what the overall aims of professional development should be and offer fragmented opportunities instead. Additionally, teacher appraisal in the region appears to further exacerbate this issue because evaluations of teacher effectiveness do not always identify teachers' strengths and weaknesses. As a result, teachers who may need support in using adaptive instruction might be trained in unrelated topics or not receive any training at all. Finally, professional development in the region is often linked with teacher compensation and promotion in ways that can incentivise teachers to view participating in training as a box ticking exercise, rather than activities designed to make them better teachers.

Policy implications

Improve access to professional development opportunities

Findings from UNICEF-OECD policy reviews reveal that several barriers might be preventing more teachers from participating in professional development. One important issue is funding. Although teacher salaries are generally low, teachers can be largely responsible for financing their own professional development, which is the case in Romania (Kitchen et al., 2017[6]). These situations can exacerbate inequity, as teachers from more socio-economically advantaged areas might be able raise more funds for training than teachers in more disadvantaged areas. Another related issue is the proximity of training providers. In Georgia, participation in professional development is publicly subsidised, but training sites can be far from where teachers live. In these cases, teachers must pay for their own travel and accommodations and arrange to cover their teaching responsibilities (Li et al., 2019[4]). Schools can help support teachers in these cases, such as by finding substitute teachers, but this type of support is not always offered. According to TALIS 2018 data, lower secondary teachers in Kazakhstan and Turkey report that there is lack of employer support to help them participate in professional development (OECD, 2019[5]).

EECA countries are undertaking several measures to make professional development more accessible. For example, Bulgaria provides government funding directly to schools to help teachers participate in professional development (forthcoming review). As part of its 2017-23 Teacher Strategy, Turkey is constructing new teacher academies around the country to make professional development opportunities easier to reach (Kitchen et al., 2019[20]). Technology can also be a useful tool for increasing access to professional development. In response to the COVID-19 pandemic, a number of professional development providers in Bulgaria now offer training digitally, and the government has removed the requirement that training be held in person (forthcoming review).

Raise the quality and relevance of professional development

Evidence from PISA and UNICEF-OECD policy reviews reveal that teachers who do participate in professional development do not necessarily demonstrate better practice. This finding suggests that EECA countries should take steps not only to make professional development accessible, but also to ensure that the training that teachers receive is relevant and effective. Developing such assurance measures is particularly important in the EECA region as increasing the number of training providers across vast areas can raise issues around training quality.

One important method that many OECD countries employ to assure the quality of professional development is to establish rigorous accreditation procedures for training providers. These procedures help link training to specific knowledge and skills outlined in teacher standards and can help coordinate the offers of non-state providers (e.g. from private and non-profit sectors) (OECD, 2013[16]). Many EECA countries have created accreditation standards and processes. As previously mentioned, Turkey plans to open several teacher academies to improve access to professional development; the government is also creating accreditation standards for these new academies to help ensure their quality (Kitchen et al., 2019[20]). Georgia recently established the Teacher Professional Development Centre to oversee teacher professional development in the country. In addition to accrediting training opportunities, the Centre has led many efforts to improve the quality of professional development, such as the Georgia Primary Education Project (G-PRIED), which trained almost 20 000 teachers in using modern pedagogical techniques (Li et al., 2019[4]). This project was particularly effective because it situated the training in school environments where teachers work on a daily basis (ibid).

Furthermore, the types of job-embedded, school-based professional learning that many OECD countries promote, and that are shown by research to be particularly effective in helping teachers adopt new methods, is lacking in some EECA countries (Kitchen et al., 2017[6]). Similarly, despite high rates of mentoring, these relationships in the region are not always structured and well resourced, which is important to making practice-centred, teacher-led professional development impactful (OECD, 2020[21]). Governments in the region can consider strengthening these school-based approaches to professional development in order to help improve teacher practice.

Adopt holistic approaches to teacher appraisal to more accurately identify professional development needs

To direct training resources efficiently, teachers need to have accurate appraisals of their competences. Evidence from PISA and UNICEF-OECD policy reviews highlight the need to promote a more balanced approach to evaluating teacher quality in the EECA region. In particular, indicators and techniques used to measure teacher effectiveness need to go beyond student results in academic competitions (e.g. international Olympiads) and on summative tests (Box 3.2), and how much teachers engage in activities that might not be related to student learning (e.g., Georgia's appraisal process verifies, among other criteria, whether teachers have written blog posts) (Li et al., 2019[4]). Teacher appraisal should instead place greater emphasis on the quality of teachers' interactions with students and their ability to create an inclusive classroom environment where each student is encouraged to achieve their potential.

> Box 3.2. Using student assessment to appraise teachers
>
> Data from PISA show that in EECA countries 84% of students are in schools whose principal reported that student assessments are used to make judgements about teachers' effectiveness, almost double the OECD average (Figure 3.12). All EECA countries have values greater than the OECD average, and Kazakhstan has the highest such percentage among all PISA-participating countries (almost 100%). Compared to more authentic measures of teacher effectiveness, this metric is particularly problematic because it is shaped by students' background, their previous preparation and other circumstances that are beyond the teacher's control. Using student assessment results to judge teacher effectiveness can be especially unfair towards teachers who teach more disadvantaged students, and it could incentivise teachers to help high-achieving students excel rather than helping all students learn.
>
> Figure 3.12. Use of student assessment to evaluate teachers
>
> Percentage of students in schools whose principal reported that student assessments are used to make judgements about teachers' effectiveness
>
>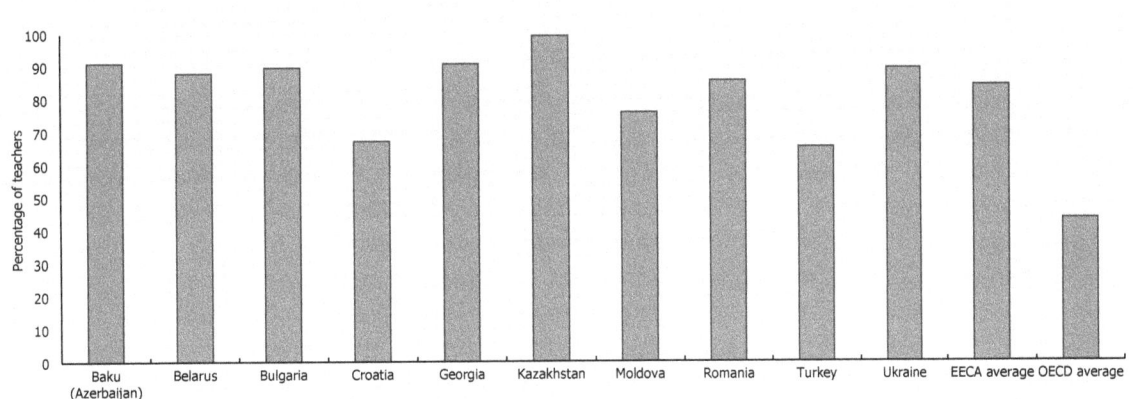
>
> Notes: In Baku (Azerbaijan) 50-75% of the sample is covered.
> The data for these figures were collected before Costa Rica became an OECD member.
> Source: (OECD, 2019[14]), *PISA 2018 database*, Table V.B1.8.1, https://www.oecd.org/pisa/data/2018database/ (accessed 17 November 2020).
>
> StatLink ▬ https://stat.link/n8khaz

There are several policy options that EECA countries can consider in order to promote a more authentic appraisal of teacher quality. First, the appraisal process and associated tools need to reinforce a more holistic approach. Many countries in the region, such as Kazakhstan, have made classroom observations mandatory in the appraisal process as they are one of the most authentic tools used internationally to assess teachers (OECD, 2013[16]). However, UNICEF and the OECD have recommended that such observations be conducted continuously (not only when teachers are appraised) so teachers can be consistently made aware of their performance and how to improve (OECD, 2020[12]). EECA countries are also more strongly integrating school-based staff in the appraisal process in addition to external actors, which can help ensure that an evaluation of a teacher effectiveness is made by those who are most knowledgeable about the teacher and his/her context (OECD, 2013[16]). In Bulgaria, for example, a school-based pedagogical council plays a significant role in the regular appraisal process (forthcoming review).

Another way to improve the how teachers are appraised, and thus the relevance of the professional development to which they are directed, is to develop the instructional leadership skills of school principals as they are often central in teacher appraisal processes. Developing the principal role in this way is very challenging and measures should focus on all aspects of their career, including their recruitment, training, evaluation, continuous improvement, and giving principals time to improve. For example, Kazakhstan has created a Master's level programme in educational leadership at the prestigious Nazarbayev University to help with principal recruitment and initial training (OECD, 2020[27]). While it is the only such programme in the country, and developing similar programmes at other universities would be helpful, this effort nevertheless serves as an example of a promising approach because it signifies the importance of the principal role and that the country is investing considerable resources into developing it.

Review teacher compensation packages to strengthen the link between professional development and improving practice

To encourage teachers to seek professional development, many countries link participating in training with greater compensation and/or promotion along a performance-based career path (OECD, 2013[16]). Several EECA countries adopt a similar approach. In Kazakhstan, participating in professional development is compulsory for teachers to maintain employment, be promoted and increase their salaries (OECD, 2019[5]). In Georgia, engaging in professional development activities represents one way (though not the only way) of accumulating credits, which are needed for teachers to be promoted to the senior levels of the country's career structure (Li et al., 2019[4]). While these measures are generally positive, the context of teaching in EECA countries can potentially distort how teachers engage with professional development.

Teacher base salaries are comparatively lower than international benchmarks. In some cases, teachers are compensated according to the hours they work (the so-called *stavka* system) (OECD/The World Bank, 2015[26]), which tend to be lower in the EECA region (see Chapter 2). In response, many countries have established complex systems of recognised supplementary activities through which teachers can augment their compensation (participating in professional development is often one of these activities) (OECD, 2017[7]; Kitchen et al., 2017[6]). In such an environment, teachers can be motivated to engage in training in order to earn more compensation, rather than to improve their practice. Georgian authorities have remarked that their system of credit accumulation has sometimes led to credit hunting behaviour from teachers, instead of encouraging teachers to focus on how to help students learn (Li et al., 2019[4])

Many EECA countries are reviewing how teachers are compensated to better align their incentives for engaging in training with the aims of professional development. In 2019, Azerbaijan increased teacher salaries by around 20% on average (Kerimkhanov, 2019[28]). Georgia has continuously increased teachers' base salary to reflect their total workload, and not just their teaching hours, which can help lessen their motivation to participate in quick win training activities. Compensating teachers more competitively can also help decrease their incentives to provide private tutoring, which can help contribute to greater educational equity (OECD, 2017[7]).

References

European CommissionEACEA/Eurydice (2020), *Compulsory Education in Europe – 2020/21*, Publications Office of the European Union, Luxembourg, http://dx.doi.org/10.2797/20126. [19]

GTC Scotland (2012), *Code of Professionalism and Conduct*, The General Teaching Council for Scotland, Edinburgh, http://www.GTcS.orG.uk (accessed on 24 June 2020). [22]

Hanushek, E. (2011), "The economic value of higher teacher quality", *Economics of Education Review*, Vol. 30/3, pp. 466-479, http://dx.doi.org/10.1016/J.ECONEDUREV.2010.12.006. [1]

Hattie, J. (2009), *Visible learning : a synthesis of over 800 meta-analyses relating to achievement*, Routledge. [2]

Ingvarson, L. (2002), *Development of a national standards framework for the teaching profession*, Australian Council for Educational Research Publishing, http://research.acer.edu.au/teaching_standards (accessed on 5 January 2018). [17]

Jacobs, G. and H. Toh-Heng (2013), "Small Steps Towards Student-Centred Learning", in *Proceedings of the International Conference on Managing the Asian Century*, Springer Singapore, http://dx.doi.org/10.1007/978-981-4560-61-0_7. [9]

Kerimkhanov, A. (2019), *Azerbaijan increases teachers' salaries by 20 pct in 2019*, Azernews, https://www.azernews.az/nation/160375.html (accessed on 25 May 2021). [28]

Kitchen, H. et al. (2019), *OECD Reviews of Evaluation and Assessment in Education: Student Assessment in Turkey*, OECD Reviews of Evaluation and Assessment in Education, OECD Publishing, Paris, https://dx.doi.org/10.1787/5edc0abe-en. [20]

Kitchen, H. et al. (2019), *OECD Reviews of Evaluation and Assessment in Education: Student Assessment in Turkey*, OECD Reviews of Evaluation and Assessment in Education, OECD Publishing, Paris, https://dx.doi.org/10.1787/5edc0abe-en. [24]

Kitchen, H. et al. (2017), *Romania*, OECD Reviews of Evaluation and Assessment in Education, OECD Publishing, Paris, https://dx.doi.org/10.1787/9789264274051-en. [6]

Li, R. et al. (2019), *OECD Reviews of Evaluation and Assessment in Education: Georgia*, OECD Reviews of Evaluation and Assessment in Education, OECD Publishing, Paris, https://dx.doi.org/10.1787/94dc370e-en. [4]

Ministry of Education of the Republic of Belarus (2019), *Approval of Instruction on the Amount, Order and Conditions for Setting Salary Supplements for Education Workers of State Budget Organisations*, https://pravo.by/upload/docs/op/W21933812_1548882000.pdf. [25]

Ministry of Education of the Republic of Belarus (2011), *Job qualifications*, http://trb.roo-stolin.gov.by/%D1%83%D1%87%D0%B8%D1%82%D0%B5%D0%BB%D1%8C%D1%81%D0%BA%D0%B0%D1%8F/%D0%B0%D1%82%D1%82%D0%B5%D1%81%D1%82%D0%B0%D1%86%D0%B8%D1%8F/%D0%BA%D0%B2%D0%B0%D0%BB%D0%B8%D1%84%D0%B8%D0%BA%D0%B0%D1%86%D0%B8%D0%BE%D0%BD%D0%BD%D1%8B%D0%B5-%D1%85%D0%B0%D1%80%D0%B0%D0%BA%D1%82%D0%B5%D1%80%D0%B8%D1%81%D1%82%D0%B8%D0%BA%D0%B8-%D0%B4%D0%BE%D0%BB%D0%B6%D0%BD%D0%BE%D1%81%D1%82%D0%B5%D0%B9 (accessed on 12 April 2021). [18]

OECD (2020), "Developing a school evaluation framework to drive school improvement", *OECD Education Policy Perspectives*, No. 26, OECD Publishing, Paris, https://dx.doi.org/10.1787/60b471de-en. [27]

OECD (2020), *Education in the Western Balkans: Findings from PISA*, PISA, OECD Publishing, Paris. [15]

OECD (2020), "Raising the quality of initial teacher education and support for early career teachers in Kazakhstan", *OECD Education Policy Perspectives*, No. 25, OECD Publishing, Paris, https://dx.doi.org/10.1787/68c45a81-en. [12]

OECD (2020), *Raising the quality of initial teacher education and support for early career teachers in Kazakhstan*, https://www.oecd-ilibrary.org/education/raising-the-quality-of-initial-teacher-education-and-support-for-early-career-teachers-in-kazakhstan_68c45a81-en (accessed on 19 April 2021). [21]

OECD (2019), *A Flying Start: Improving Initial Teacher Preparation Systems*, OECD Publishing, Paris, https://dx.doi.org/10.1787/cf74e549-en. [11]

OECD (2019), *PISA 2018 Results (Volume I): What Students Know and Can Do*, PISA, OECD Publishing, Paris, https://dx.doi.org/10.1787/5f07c754-en. [14]

OECD (2019), *PISA 2018 Results (Volume III): What School Life Means for Students' Lives*, PISA, OECD Publishing, Paris, https://dx.doi.org/10.1787/acd78851-en. [13]

OECD (2019), *TALIS 2018 Results (Volume I): Teachers and School Leaders as Lifelong Learners*, TALIS, OECD Publishing, Paris, https://dx.doi.org/10.1787/1d0bc92a-en. [5]

OECD (2019), *Working and Learning Together: Rethinking Human Resource Policies for Schools*, OECD Reviews of School Resources, OECD Publishing, Paris, https://dx.doi.org/10.1787/b7aaf050-en. [23]

OECD (2017), *OECD Reviews of Integrity in Education: Ukraine 2017*, OECD Publishing, Paris, https://dx.doi.org/10.1787/9789264270664-en. [7]

OECD (2013), *Synergies for Better Learning: An International Perspective on Evaluation and Assessment*, OECD Reviews of Evaluation and Assessment in Education, OECD Publishing, Paris, https://dx.doi.org/10.1787/9789264190658-en. [16]

OECD (2012), *Equity and Quality in Education: Supporting Disadvantaged Students and Schools*, OECD Publishing, Paris, https://dx.doi.org/10.1787/9789264130852-en. [10]

OECD/The World Bank (2015), *OECD Reviews of School Resources: Kazakhstan 2015*, OECD Reviews of School Resources, OECD Publishing, Paris, https://dx.doi.org/10.1787/9789264245891-en. [26]

Peterson, A. et al. (2018), "Understanding innovative pedagogies: Key themes to analyse new approaches to teaching and learning", *OECD Education Working Papers*, No. 172, OECD Publishing, Paris, https://dx.doi.org/10.1787/9f843a6e-en. [8]

Rivkin, S., E. Hanushek and J. Kain (2005), "Teachers, Schools, and Academic Achievement", *Econometrica*, Vol. 73/2, pp. 417-458, http://dx.doi.org/10.1111/j.1468-0262.2005.00584.x. [3]

Notes

[1] To account for differences in response style across countries and economies (e.g. if students from a country tend to respond more positively or negatively in general), OECD analysts adjusted the value of each individual index according to the average response across all indices.

[2] Since only one Western Balkan economy took the PISA teacher questionnaire in 2018, this paper does not discuss teachers' own experiences with ITE.

[3] Level of qualification refers to Bachelor's degree, Master's degree, or doctoral degree.

www.ingramcontent.com/pod-product-compliance
Ingram Content Group UK Ltd.
Pitfield, Milton Keynes, MK11 3LW, UK
UKHW051300180426
11947UKWH00020B/1816